THE CHOIC

DIGITAL
PHOTOGRAPHY

*We must remember that a photograph
can hold just as much as we put into it,
and no one has ever approached the
full possibilities of the medium.*

Ansel Adams 1902–1984

THE CHOICE GUIDE TO

DIGITAL
PHOTOGRAPHY

MARGARET BROWN

www.choice.com.au

CHOICEBOOKS

Australian Consumers' Association

CHOICEBOOKS
Copyright © Margaret Brown 2004

Published by
CHOICE Books
57 Carrington Road
Marrickville NSW 2204 Australia
www.choice.com.au

National Library of Australia
Cataloguing-in-publication data

Brown, Margaret.
    The Choice guide to digital photography.

    Includes index.
    ISBN 1 920705 31 7.

    1. Photography - Digital techniques. 2. Digital cameras.
    3. Image processing - Digital techniques. I. Australian
    Consumers' Association. II. Title.

    771.33

Edited by Colette Batha
Cover design by Howard Binns-McDonald
Cover photos by Margaret Brown
Except where indicated, all photos by Margaret Brown
Typeset in Australia by Midland Typesetters
Printed in Australia by Griffin Press

10 9 8 7 6 5 4 3 2 1

Contents

Introduction

Australian and New Zealand consumers are going digital in a big way according to data collected by GfK Marketing Services, an organisation that monitors worldwide product sales in over 200 non-food categories. GfK Marketing Services has been tracking sales of photographic products since March 2001 when digital still cameras (DSCs) were much more expensive than conventional cameras. However, the market has changed considerably in the intervening years. During 2003, Australians spent almost A$2 billion on digital products and, for the first time, digital cameras outsold traditional film cameras. Digital cameras and camcorders were in demand on both sides of the Tasman Sea, with consumers in both Australia and New Zealand purchasing just over twice as many DSCs and almost 50% more digital camcorders than the previous year. This trend looks set to continue.

If you're wondering what is driving the shift towards digital photography, many factors have combined to make the purchase of a digital camera attractive to a wide variety of consumers. For a start, the total number of households with computers is rising steadily with just over 70% of all Australian and New Zealand households expected to be equipped with a computer the mid 2004. Broadband Internet access is also gaining popularity for both home and business users. With roughly three-quarters of both populations using the Internet on a regular basis, either at home or at work, consumers have a strong incentive to share experiences online.

The increasing affordability of digital imaging equipment is also driving the shift to digital capture. In the year August 2003–2004

Australians purchased 655,223 digital still cameras, with a market value of almost A$3.25 billion. Average prices for a compact DSC fell by 23% and for digital SLR cameras by 51% in the same period. The year-on-year growth for compact DSCs was 85.7%, while for digital SLR cameras, it was 782%.

In addition the new cameras have many more features and functions than previous-generation cameras—and more capabilities than film camera. The incentive for consumers to purchase a digital camera rather than a film camera is strong. Then there's the 'fun' factor; digital cameras are so much more enjoyable to use than their analogue equivalents. The thrill of being able to see the picture you took immediately after taking it and sharing the experience with your companions is immediate and undeniable.

Despite the obvious advantages, digital cameras are not necessarily the best choice for everybody. Many people see digital photography as complex, expensive and highly technological. Others take such a small number of pictures in a typical year that the up-front investment in a digital camera and the accessories required to use it effectively—not to mention the time required to master the new equipment and procedures involved in obtaining digital prints—is probably not worthwhile. Fortunately, technology is stepping in to overcome some of these objections.

Most of the latest point-and-shoot digital cameras are as easy to use as film cameras, although beginners must learn to use a couple of new and quite different camera settings if they wish to obtain the best results consistently. However, much of the underlying technology is 'transparent' and you don't need special qualifications to 'drive' a digital camera. Nor do you need a computer to obtain prints from your digital photos (although having a PC lets you do more with your pictures). Most neighbourhood photolabs can produce prints from digital camera files—and they'll usually cost much the same as prints from your film camera. Furthermore, you need only print (and pay for) the pictures that 'worked' so shooting digitally could save you dollars in the long run. Finally, as these prints can be made on the same type of photographic paper as prints from film images, there's every reason for your digital shots to be as 'valuable' as those from a film camera.

Printing your own digital snapshots at home has also been made easy with the release of a new printing standard, PictBridge, which lets you connect your digital camera directly to a printer. No computer is required; you simply 'drive' the prints from your camera's viewing screen. Printers with PictBridge connections range from compact, 'push-button' models that produce credit card and snapshot sized prints to desktop printers that can deliver A3 sized enlargements and the end results can be as good as prints from a photolab. Digital photography has never been easier.

The number of things you can do with your digital pictures continues to expand as the technology develops. The recent proliferation of mobile phones with built in digicams is a case in point. So, too, is the rapidly expanding range of software applications targeting hobbies as diverse as scrapbooking, embroidery and genealogy, to name but a few. Deciding which camera to buy—and how to use it effectively—are becoming everyday problems for non-specialist consumers and it can be difficult to source objective and reliable information.

The CHOICE Guide to Digital Photography will provide you with the information you need to make well-informed decisions about all aspects of digital photography. Its aim is to open this exciting world to you and show you how to use your digital camera to take the kind of pictures you enjoy—and others appreciate. It will also provide a guide to the different types of cameras on the market so you can select the best camera for your requirements and budget. There's also advice on buying strategies that can save you money long-term.

Instructions will be provided for key editing functions that will make it easier for you to send pictures by email and obtain good-looking prints from your digital photos. We will also explore accessory items that will enhance your digital picture taking and consider new and emerging technologies (such as mobile phone cameras, picture storage systems and transfer protocols) that are impacting on digital photography now—and may have greater significance in the future. Finally, we will provide a glossary of commonly used terms to help you deal with the jargon when shopping for a digital camera or ordering digital prints.

Digital photography can be fun for all the family and it's accessible to people of all ages. All you require is a willingness to understand some new camera functions and learn how to use them and a camera to put your knowledge into practice. *The CHOICE Guide to Digital Photography* will start you on the road to success and satisfaction.

Chapter 1

A new way to take pictures

The developments that have taken place in photography over the past 30 or so years have had one primary objective: to make it easy for camera users to obtain good photos each time they press the shutter button. To that end, we've seen the development of:

- systems that measure ambient lighting and adjust the camera's exposure settings to provide correctly exposed photographs
- systems that focus the camera's lens on subjects occupying the centre of the field of view
- built-in flash units that pop up automatically in low light levels to provide additional illumination for the subject
- film that responds to a wide range of light levels and delivers sharp, grain-free prints
- printing technologies that can detect minor faults in photographs and correct them automatically before producing a print, ensuring the maximum number of satisfactory prints can be obtained from each roll of film
- preset shooting modes that minimise the number of decisions camera users have to make before taking a picture.

Because of these developments, consumers have become accustomed to low hassle, point-and-shoot photography with film-based cameras. Very little understanding of how a camera works and how the picture is created is required to use these simple cameras and anybody capable of pointing the camera at a subject and pressing the shutter release can take reasonably good pictures.

At least that's the marketing message from the camera manufacturers. In practice, understanding how films and cameras work, selecting the appropriate controls and thinking about each picture as you're composing the shot in the viewfinder will make a huge difference between whether the shot you take is good or unusable. So will your choice of photolab because, regardless of how good the equipment is, the overriding expertise of the lab operator determines whether your pictures will be correctly exposed, with natural-looking colour rendition and whether they will be free of unattractive white dust specks, fingermarks and hair lines.

The digital revolution

Until quite recently, most of us took photography for granted and enjoyed the feeling that photography was cheap, straightforward and so simple even a child could take decent pictures. It was also seen as a mature technology in which most user-related issues had been solved. Then, suddenly, up pops digital photography and the market is thrown into turmoil. It's complicated! It's highly technical! It's expensive! It's only for computer nerds!

These concerns may have been true in the early days of digital photography more than 20 years ago and were still true of many digital cameras up until about two years ago. The same can not be said today, however. During the past two years, digital photography has moved from being a technophile's pastime to something anybody can do—and there are no age or gender barriers to prevent anyone from becoming involved. The technology barriers that have hitherto deterred many people against buying a digital camera are also falling.

According to NOIE (the National Office for the Information Economy), more than 65% of Australian households have at least

The Benefits of Digital Images

There are several advantages in having your photographs in digital form:

- They are easier to share in emails or on websites.
- They are easier to store (a CD with 250 image files takes up much less space than 10 packets of prints and negatives).
- Stored digital images are easier to find and organise than photographs on film.
- Stored digital images will retain their colour integrity longer than film and print images, which normally start to change colour within 10–20 years.
- Photographs that have been stored digitally can be easily migrated to new storage systems when technology improvements have made them cost-effective.

However, there are also some negative aspects to consider:

- Digital images are easily deleted from camera memory cards and computer hard drives and, once deleted, may be lost forever. Note: some photolabs offer a file recovery service for images that have been accidentally deleted from camera memory cards, but there can be no guarantee that all files can be fully restored.
- Care is required when archiving digital images on CD. Unless they are stored and handled carefully, CDs are vulnerable to physical damage that may make them unreadable and the files on them will be lost. Note: always make at least two back-ups as insurance against CD damage.
- If you want to share digital photos via websites or emails, you must learn how to resize them (see pages 168–169) because digital images that are good enough to print will be too large to send electronically.

one home computer and roughly 60% of Australians use the Internet on a regular basis. As of June 2003, Australia had more than five million Internet subscribers (4.4 million households, and 659,000 businesses and government agencies). The ratios are similar in New Zealand, which has consistently ranked in the top 10 of the most computer-literate nations in the world for the past five years. Such high levels of computer penetration create an incentive for more people to buy a digital camera, especially since the benefits of taking digital pictures are so strongly linked to the increasing demand for computer-based tasks involving pictures. These benefits have become much more tangible as DSC prices have dropped. Some of the more significant advantages of digital photography are outlined in the box *The Benefits of Digital Images*.

The digital advantage

The rapidly growing popularity of digital cameras has thrown up a new suite of issues for consumers to embrace, including how to obtain good prints they can enjoy sharing with others. Fortunately, this is not as difficult as it appears because digital photography is similar to traditional film-based photography in many respects. Many of the solutions outlined at the beginning of this chapter, which were developed for film-based photography, have been successfully applied to digital cameras to give us point-and-shoot cameras that are easy to use and, when used correctly, can produce good pictures. But you can do so much more with a digital camera than a 35mm or APS snapshot model. The way a digital camera captures, manipulates and presents pictorial information is so different that anybody who buys a digital camera must embark on a steep learning path before they can take advantage of all the facilities a digital camera can offer.

Digital cameras have some significant advantages over film cameras.

- A picture can be viewed immediately after it has been taken allowing the user to delete unsuccessful shots and re-take them on the spot.
- Short video clips can be captured and displayed on a computer monitor or TV screen, in many cases at full screen size.
- Some cameras allow sound 'bites' to be recorded with individual still pictures. These can be played back either on the camera's monitor screen or on a PC.
- It is possible to adjust key controls, such as picture resolution and size, colour balance and sensor sensitivity, on a shot-by-shot basis to obtain the desired result, regardless of how much the lighting, subject proximity and subject movement change.
- It is possible to switch from full colour to black-and-white or sepia tone on an individual shot basis.
- The image file can be downloaded from the camera to a PC and emailed to family and friends, posted on a website or used as wallpaper on a PC screen.

No film camera supports any of these functions. In contrast, most—if not all of them—are available at the touch of a few buttons on the majority of digital cameras.

However, there are other ways to obtain digitised images from pictures taken with a non-digital camera and, if you're an infrequent photographer, they may be more cost-effective—at least temporarily (see *Why scan?* on page 128).

Should you buy?

If all the advantages outlined above are attractive, you may be in the market for a digital camera. However you may also wonder whether it's worth paying between 50% and 150% more than you would for a film camera to obtain a digital camera with similar capabilities. One of the best ways to decide whether to buy a DSC is to analyse what you currently spend on photography and how you plan to use your digital photos. Ask yourself the following questions:

One of the joys of using a digital camera is that you can immediately see the picture taken. This makes digital cameras ideal for teaching children and camera-shy adults the fun of picture-taking and helps everyone to become a better photographer.

1. How many pictures do you normally take in a month?

Photographers who take two rolls of film per month and have them processed and printed at a lab typically spend roughly A\$50 per month on film and processing services. This works out at approximately A\$600 per year, which is about the same price as a fully featured 3-megapixel DSC with a 3x optical zoom lens plus a 128 MB memory card that would allow you to store approximately 70 high-resolution pictures. If you don't print your digital photos, you could recoup your initial investment costs within 12 months.

2. How do you like to view photographs?

If your preference is for snapshot-sized prints that you can hand around or post to friends and relatives, a DSC may not be the best option—although it's easy (and, usually cost-effective) to have prints made from digital camera files at many local photolabs. However, if prints are only part of the story and you want to share your shots online, either by posting them on a website or emailing them, a DSC will simplify this process and provide a cheap way of obtaining digital pictures—plus prints for sharing.

3. Would you like to be able to include pictures in documents, such as letters, business reports or presentations?

A DSC makes this process easy; you simply download your shots, resize them (if necessary) to fit the document's requirements and import them into the document. In contrast, if you shoot with a film camera, the film has to be processed and then scanned before the pictures can be used.

4. Would you like to capture video?

Most compact DSCs allow you to capture a short video clip as an alternative to a still picture. With many cameras, these clips have low resolution and low frame rates that make them look rough and jerky when viewed on a TV screen and the cheaper cameras don't record sound with the video. However they can be viewed effectively on a computer monitor although they will only take up a small section of the screen area. Note: if video is a high priority, investing in a digital camcorder that can store still images on a removable memory card is probably a better option than buying a DSC. More information on video capture, including a comparison of the features and output of DSCs and digital camcorders, can be found in Chapter 8.

Making the change

Regardless of whether you opt to change to a digital camera for taking pictures or keep using your film camera and scan your negatives, a move into digital photography will require you to change some of the ways you approach picture taking and sharing.

7

Swapping from film-based to digital photography also poses some new problems:

- How should you store your digital pictures?
- How long will digital pictures last?
- How can you turn the image files into prints?
- What should you take to a photolab if you want them to print your shots for you?
- What kind of home printer should you buy?

The answers to these questions will be revealed in the chapters to follow.

If you decide to purchase a digital camera, you will also need a basic understanding of how it works, which means learning about new features and functions and becoming familiar with the terminology associated with digital capture. It's reassuring to know that many aspects of digital photography have parallels in film-based capture, which means very little effort is required to set you on your way. And the instant feedback a digital camera provides will help you to learn new procedures quickly. A comparison of film and digital cameras is provided in the box *Digital Photography Differences*.

Digital Photography Differences

Although most people are familiar with traditional cameras and many can use them with reasonable confidence, the same can't be said of digital cameras. Digital cameras carry a hint of complexity and involvement with computer technology, which can make anyone with limited computer experience and technological confidence shy away. However, although there's more to learn when shooting with a digital camera, the technology is more forgiving and your mistakes are usually easy to recover from, which means you soon become a much better picture-taker.

Film and digital cameras share many of the same features—a light-tight body, lens and shutter button. Similarly, all photographs consist of tiny elements: from the grains of silver or micro-clouds of colour dye in film photography to the ink dots in newspaper photos to the picture elements ('pixels') in a digital image. However, the way the picture is captured by each type of camera is radically different and the pictures are used somewhat differently. In a traditional camera, light falling on the film creates tiny chemical changes, which are amplified by the development process to create a negative or slide. In a digital camera, the film is replaced by an image sensor. This is a slice of silicon that carries millions of light-sensitive photodiodes. Each photodiode produces an electrical signal in proportion to the amount of light it receives. The resulting electrical signal is passed to the camera's microprocessor, which creates the digital image from the captured information and then stores it in the camera's memory. (A schematic diagram showing how this is done can be found on the first page of the colour insert.)

Because no chemical processing is required—and the digital image processing is carried out within the camera straight after the picture is taken—a digital photograph can be viewed on the spot, immediately after it's been taken. This is a huge advantage to photographers as they can see whether the shot was successful and, if not, shoot it again. Thanks to this instant feedback, most digital photographers learn quickly what to do and what not to do. This is a very 'painless' way to improve your photography.

In-camera image processing has some additional advantages because it allows you to change some hitherto unalterable parameters on a shot-by-shot basis. Whereas with a film camera, loading a film locked you into a particular output type (print or slide, black-and-white or colour), with a digital camera you can elect to take a full-colour shot or choose between black-and-white and, often, sepia (for an old-fashioned look) on a shot-by-shot basis. Some DSCs even let you add colour effects and a few will capture in negative, 'posterised' or 'solarised' formats.

Similarly, whereas loading a film locks you into a preset sensitivity, with a digital camera you can adjust the gain of the sensor each time you take a photo. Thus, when you go from bright daylight (where an ISO 50 or 100 setting is appropriate) into deep shade it's easy to change the ISO setting on the camera to 400 (or faster) so you can take pictures that aren't blurred by camera shake. Moving from daylight into indoor lighting can be doubly problematic with a film camera because most films are designed for outdoor lighting and don't produce accurate colour when used with other lighting types. With a digital camera, the white balance control lets you adjust the colour balance in a shot to compensate for a variety of colour casts and, again, this can be done on a shot-by-shot basis.

A few DSCs also let you crop the picture and resave it, using the camera's controls. This can improve a poorly composed shot or allow you to 'zoom' in closer on a subject that was too far away to make a good picture with the zoom lens fully extended. Care is required with this function, which will be explained in detail in Chapter 5.

Picture quality

The question that concerns most newcomers to digital photography is: will the pictures from a digital camera produce prints that look and feel like real photos? Until a few years ago, the answer ranged from 'no' to a qualified 'maybe' but today, it's a definite 'yes'. However, there's a proviso: digital cameras can match (or even better) many film cameras' output as long as users shoot with the highest resolution and quality settings. If you take 24 digital pictures to a photolab on a 1.4 MB floppy disk, their output quality will be so low most labs will refuse to print them as it's a waste of paper and processing chemistry. In contrast, if you have taken shots with a 3-megapixel (or higher) camera at the highest resolution and quality settings, most photolabs should be able to produce snapshot-sized prints that are indistinguishable from prints from film.

The key to successful digital photography lies in knowing what camera settings to use and how much different-sized image files can be enlarged for printing. If you keep to the tried-and-tested print size parameters (outlined in Chapter 2) and have your photo printed at a competent and quality-focused photolab or on a good desktop photo printer, your digital images should have all the sharpness and tonal nuances of a photograph taken on film—and, in some cases, they could well be better than film-based photographs.

Interesting Fact #1

Digital camera technology has evolved from the technology used to produce TV images and relies on an electronic sensor and data processing system to produce pictures. The first digital still camera, the Mavica, was released by Sony in August 1981. Essentially a video camera that took 'freeze-frame' stills, it recorded image data onto a mini-disk, which was inserted into a video reader. Pictures were displayed on a TV set.

In 1991, Kodak released the first professional digital camera system, based on a Nikon F3 film camera fitted with a 1.3-megapixel, Kodak-developed sensor. This camera was aimed at photojournalists and produced printable pictures that were suitable for reproduction in newspapers. The first consumer digital camera was the Apple Quick-Take 100, which was released in February 1994. With VGA (640 x 480 pixels) resolution and a binocular-style body, it was the fore-runner of today's digital still cameras.

Chapter 2

Buying a digital still camera

Choosing a digital camera should be easy but, unfortunately, it isn't. The market is a complex one and most camera manufacturers have introduced new types of cameras, new capabilities and new 'form factors' (body shapes), especially in the past 12–18 months. To complicate matters, individual camera models tend to have much shorter market life spans than comparable film cameras. It is common for manufacturers to replace a model that has sold successfully for six to eight months with a new model with similar features which has been given minor cosmetic and functional enhancements. Consequently, consumers are faced with a large number of cameras to choose from and minimal information about the key factors that should influence their choice.

Camera types

The digital camera market is split into four main types: compact DSCs, digital SLRs, digital camcorders and camera-equipped peripheral devices. These categories can be further subdivided.

Compact DSCs

Also known as 'digicams', these range from the tiny 'visual note-taker' units that can slip into a pocket, through small-sized point-and-shoot models to sophisticated 'prosumer' (or semi-professional) cameras with high-resolution sensors and large, high-quality lenses. Sensor resolutions range from around 3 mega-pixels to 8 megapixels, which means the entry-level models can capture shots that make excellent snapshot-sized prints, while the high-end models produce images that can be enlarged to poster size. The main sub-groups in this sector are:

Visual note-takers

These ultra-compact models are designed to be as portable as your mobile phone, allowing you to capture pictures spontaneously wherever you are. Most will fit into a shirt pocket; few have zoom lenses and some lack removable memory cards. If a built-in flash is provided, the light it emits seldom covers more than 1.5 metres. Many models come with docking stations that make downloading pictures and charging the camera's battery very simple. Video capture, if supported, is usually at low resolution and clip lengths tend to be short. A few models support voice recording.

Casio's ultra-slim Exilim EX-S100 is a typical 'visual note-taker' camera.

Compact point-and-shoot digicams

These models are structurally similar to compact point-and-shoot film cameras and offer the best combination of price, features and ease-of-use for most buyers. The range is huge, from under A$300 for full-auto models with fixed focus lenses to over A$1000 for a high-resolution camera with a zoom lens (normally with 3x magnification) and extensive manual controls. Some cameras in this category feature innovative styling, while others offer novel functions like 3-D capture and voice annotation. Most have slots for removable memory cards, although some come with 8–32 MB of internal memory and may not be supplied with a memory card. A few models have slots for two different card types.

The compact Ricoh Caplio GX has similar controls and functions to most point-and-shoot digicams but has a 3x wide-angle zoom lens that can focus down to one centimetre.

Prosumer cameras with non-interchangeable lenses

These models are typically priced from around A$1200 to well over A$2000. Designed for serious photographers, they provide users with full creative control over the colours and tonal values in the pictures they take and normally include at least as many functions as 35mm film SLR cameras. Most are fitted with high-quality, extended-range (5x or more) zoom lenses and high-resolution (5- to 8-megapixel or more) sensors. All have built-in flash units, many with adjustable flash output, and most have 'hot-shoe' fittings that accept accessory flash units. All cameras in this category use removable media and most are supplied with at least 32 MB cards. Most can record video clips with sound—sometimes at quite high quality—and many allow you to record short voice memos which can be either attached to a still image file or stored as independent 'sound bites' in the camera's memory.

Canon's 7.1-megapixel PowerShot G6 combines a high-quality lens with a wide variety of user-adjustable controls and produces high-resolution photographs.

Digital single-lens reflex (DSLR) cameras

These fall into two categories, those with interchangeable lenses and those without. However, with the release of a number of under-A$2500 interchangeable-lens models since late 2003, most camera manufacturers have ceased development of DSLRs with fixed lenses. These cameras are increasingly being integrated into the 'prosumer' DSC category.

Interchangeable-lens DSLRs

These cameras look and operate like 35mm film SLR cameras and frequently use the same lenses, although usually with an adjustment to the effective lens angle of view. The category covers cameras designed for both enthusiast and professional photographers and prices typically range from around A$2000 to over A$10 000, depending on the quality of the camera body and the size of the image sensor. By the end of 2004, the leading SLR camera manufacturers (Canon, Konica Minolta, Nikon, Pentax and Sigma) had at least one under-A$2500 model on sale that could use existing 35mm SLR lenses. Canon and Pentax also had models priced below A$2000 in this category. Olympus, which released its first DSLR, the E-1, in late 2003, is the only DSLR manufacturer with cameras that cannot use existing Olympus lenses (although adaptors are available overseas). Olympus released its first under-A$2000 DSLR model, the E-300, at the end of 2004 and, at the same time, increased its range of compatible lenses from six to nine.

Konica Minolta's new Dynax 7D can use existing Minolta lenses and is compatible with new digital lenses from Konica Minolta and other lens manufacturers.

Zoom-lens reflex-style (ZLR) cameras

This category is similar to the prosumer cameras with non-interchangeable lenses group in supporting a wide range of user-adjustable controls and functions and having very high-resolution sensors (8-megapixel sensors are available in most current models). The main difference between the two categories lies in the viewing system. In older examples of this type of camera, the viewfinder was connected to the lens by a reflecting pentaprism/mirror system or series of mirrors so the photographer saw the same view of the subject that the lens picked up. Recently, manufacturers have replaced the reflecting pentaprism/mirror systems with electronic viewfinders, which also show the subject as the lens 'sees' it, but are cheaper to manufacture and weigh considerably less.

Nikon's Coolpix 8400 combines a high-resolution (8-megapixel) sensor with a high-quality zoom lens, electronic viewfinder and wide range of user-adjustable functions.

Webcams and mobile phone/PDA cameras

These imaging devices belong in a totally new category that has no film camera equivalent and, in many cases, picture-taking is a subsidiary function to the main purpose of the device. The cameras are very small and most have low-resolution sensors and a limited range of functions. The pictures captured by most

Sony Ericsson's 1.3-megapixel S700i camera phone represents a totally new type of picture-taking device.

models on the current market are only suitable for online use but they can be fun and may be useful for some business applications. The release of the first 1-megapixel mobile phone/camera in March 2004 signalled some potential for development in this market. In parts of Asia, where the communications infra-structure supports high bandwidth applications, phones with 2-megapixel sensors can record and send movie clips. Many also come with removable memory cards (128 MB or more), built-in flash units, GPS (global positioning system) and 2G or 3G mobile internet connection.

Choosing a camera

When shopping for a digital camera, look first at how the camera is likely to be used. What types of pictures do you plan to take? How do you plan to view them? Do you want to make prints or just post your snapshots on a website or attach them to emails? Will you be using the camera to take holiday snapshots or simply as a replace-ment for the family's film camera?

Then consider who will use the camera. Will it be used by the entire family or only one person? What is the level of photographic expertise and computer literacy of the main user? What are the user's expectations and limitations? How open are they to learning new things?

Finally, consider your budget. In mid 2003, a typical compact DSC cost roughly 60% more (on average) than a film camera with the same performance specifications. However by mid 2004, the price difference was reduced to around 40% and further declines can be expected, although probably quite slowly. DSLR cameras currently cost 60–70% more than their film equivalents and this disparity is likely to continue for the foreseeable future. Essentially consumers should expect a digital camera to remain more expen-sive than an equivalent film camera for some time to come. You will also need to allow at least A$200 extra to the basic cost of the camera for additional memory to ensure you can enjoy using the camera and have the capacity to take plenty of pictures.

Picture-based choices

If you just want to take pictures for sharing online, almost any digital camera will do, but if you want to make snapshot-sized prints you will need a camera with at least 2-megapixel resolution. For slightly larger prints, a 3-megapixel digicam will allow you to print at A5 size with photo quality and a 4-megapixel camera will give you photo quality A4 prints. However, you will only be able to achieve these objectives by shooting with the highest resolution and quality settings.

The following table lists the recommended maximum print sizes you can obtain from cameras and camcorders with different sensor resolutions when pictures are taken with highest resolution and quality settings (see Chapter 5 for more information on these functions).

Sensor resolution (megapixels)	Image size (pixels)	Maximum print size
0.3	640 x 480	Not recommended for printing (emails only)
0.8	1024 x 768	10.5 x 7.0 cm
1.92	1600 x 1200	13 x 9 cm
2.1	1800 x 1200	15 x 10 cm
3.1	2048 x 1536	17.25 x 13 cm
4.0	2272 x 1704	19.2 x 14.4 cm
5.0	2560 x 1920	21.25 x 15.95 cm
6.2	3072 x 2068	35.6 x 28 cm
13.5	4500 x 3000	50.8 x 40.6 cm

Source: *Digital Camera Pocket Guide*, Media Publishing, 2003.
www.photoreview.com.au

Batteries

All digital cameras rely on a ready supply of electrical power to function and all are supplied with batteries. The type of battery a camera uses can affect its usability so it's worth considering it when choosing a camera. Essentially, two types of batteries are used: rechargeable and non-rechargeable. In the former case, some cameras use proprietary lithium-ion batteries, while others use rechargeable AA or AAA NiMH (nickel metal hydride) cells. Cameras that are supplied with non-rechargeable AA or AAA batteries can normally also work with rechargeable NiMH batteries of the same size. Because digital cameras are quite power-hungry, this is generally more cost-effective for users than buying non-rechargeable batteries on a regular basis, especially if you use your camera frequently. Note: it is wise to purchase at least two sets of rechargeable batteries to ensure you are not caught without power. Keep them topped up as rechargeable batteries lose charge slowly during storage.

Power consumption varies greatly between cameras. However three years of camera testing for *Photo Review Australia* has shown steady improvements in power usage across the board, although the cheaper models that use AA batteries tend to lag well behind cameras that use rechargeable lithium-ion batteries in power economy. Recently released models that use lithium-ion batteries should allow you to take at least 100 shots on a single charge. You can extend that by turning off the LCD monitor and using the viewfinder to compose shots (LCD screens use a high proportion of the camera's energy budget).

The advantage of having a camera that uses AA or AAA batteries is that you can always find replacement batteries, wherever you are. If your camera uses lithium-ion batteries and you plan to be away from mains power for a long period of time (more than two or three days), buying a spare battery is advisable. Always remove the batteries from the camera when you know you won't be using it for a week or two. This protects the camera from accidental leakage. Over time, rechargeable batteries lose their ability to accept charge. Most remain usable for between 300 and 500 cycles. When they 'die', return them to a camera or electrical store for recycling.

User-based choices

If you're short on technical know-how or want a camera the entire family can use, look for a model with a simple control suite and clear, easily read menu system. The latter is also vital for anybody with poor vision, while those with limited dexterity will require a camera with reasonably large control buttons. Note: large buttons are almost impossible to find on small cameras so you may have difficulty meeting this requirement.

Keen photographers who have used a film SLR camera will be best suited to a digital SLR, despite that fact that many high-resolution digicams with non-interchangeable lenses support more user-adjustable functions. Most DSLRs are so similar in their layout and shooting controls to 35mm SLR cameras that the changeover to digital becomes almost seamless and some DSLR models are now priced well below the top models in the 'prosumer' DSC category. If you already have an interchangeable-lens film SLR camera kit with two or more lenses made by Canon, Minolta, Nikon or Pentax, you should be able to find an under-A$2500 DSLR that can use your 35mm SLR's lenses.

Travellers are likely to be attracted by ultra-compact models that are small enough to slip into a purse or pocket. Light weight is an important factor for backpackers and cameras that are easy to conceal make their owners less likely targets for theft. Some caution should be exercised when choosing a small camera as small buttons can be difficult to adjust when you're wearing gloves or in a hurry. Ultra-compact DSCs may also have a limited range of functions. Batteries can also be an issue for these cameras (see the box on batteries).

One important decision you will need to make is whether you want to capture video clips with your DSC and, if so, how you plan to use them. This can influence your choice of camera types (DSLRs cannot record video clips) and provide a basis for selecting one camera model over another. This issue is covered in detail in Chapter 8.

Shopping Tips

Although everybody seeks out bargains, shopping around for the cheapest price is not always the best strategy when buying a digital camera. In many cases you may be able to obtain a better all-round deal by paying a few dollars more and purchasing your camera from a specialist retailer whose staff understand the technology and are prepared to spend time demonstrating a selection of cameras to you. Be flexible in your budgeting to cover the added necessities required to make your camera as usable as your film camera. Tip: Allow A$100–A$250 for a high-capacity memory card plus, perhaps, some of the additional items outlined in points 5 and 6 below.

If you follow the strategy outlined below when buying a digital camera, you should end up with a camera that is comfortable to operate, easy to use and capable of taking the types of pictures you want. Do your homework before you start shopping so you have a good idea about what you want and how much it should cost.

If you're looking for a bargain, keep an eye on product life cycles. Most DSCs remain in the market for between six and nine months before being replaced by a new model that may vary only slightly from the model it replaces. If you know a new model is due, there's a good chance shop staff will also have this information and you may be able to negotiate a lower price for your camera or have some valuable add-ons included for the published price. A visit to www.photoreview.com.au will alert you to new cameras entering the Australian market.

When shopping for a DSC or digital camcorder, focus on the following issues:

1. Have a reasonably good idea of the type of camera you want and the most suitable resolution and zoom range for your purposes *before* you start shopping.
2. Decide how much money you are prepared to invest in your camera.
3. Make a list of the features you'd like. The latest digital cameras have plenty of useful functions. They can record short video clips or action sequences, stitch pictures together to make panoramas, shoot extreme close-ups and add sound annotations to pictures. Some can double as voice recorders and a few models come with communications capabilities such as Bluetooth antennas and Internet support.
4. Decide how much manual control you want. Snap shooters will find a camera with full-auto operation is fine most of the time, but manual overrides are essential if you like to control the camera's focus, lens aperture and shutter speeds. Many higher-resolution DSCs provide aperture priority and shutter priority auto exposure modes that parallel the settings on most 35mm SLR cameras.
5. Match the build of the camera to its intended use. If you plan to carry the camera in your pocket, check the body's

sealing and favour models with fully retractable lenses. Well-sealed camera bodies and lenses that withdraw right into the camera body behind protective lens covers will ensure dust and lint are excluded. Waterproof cameras have bodies that are designed to survive immersion (though not necessarily depths over 1–2 metres), while water-resistant cameras can survive a few spots of rain but not necessarily a drenching. If you're a bushwalker, consider a waterproof housing as it will protect the camera against both water and dust (although it will add to the overall weight you have to carry).

6. Look for useful bundled items, such as a high-capacity memory card (at least 256 MB is advisable for a 4-megapixel camera), rechargeable batteries and a charger, a docking station, carry pouch and editing software (see useful add-ons below).

7. Buy from a shop where the staff is prepared to spend time with you and take an interest in your purchase. Avoid 'box-shifters'. A DSC is a complex piece of technology and there are so many types to choose from that it's easy to become confused. It's worth paying a few extra dollars to know you've bought a camera that will truly meet your needs and that you're comfortable using. Don't buy a camera that doesn't feel comfortable in your hands!

Useful add-ons

Although your camera should be supplied with everything you need to start taking pictures, research in the USA has shown most DSC buyers return to shops within two to four weeks of the initial purchase to buy additional items they need to use their camera more effectively. Top of the list is a high-capacity memory card because the cards supplied with most DSCs are often limited to storing fewer than 10 high-resolution shots. (In some cases, the supplied card can't even accommodate one high-resolution file!) When buying additional memory, aim for a card that will hold at least one film's worth (24–36 shots) of pictures taken with the camera's highest resolution and quality settings. For a 3-megapixel camera, this means a 128 MB card; for a 5-megapixel camera with TIFF or RAW capture, 256 MB or higher will be required. Appendix 1 shows a table of recent prices for memory cards. This table is regularly updated on the *Photo Review* website at www.photoreview.com.au. Note: the memory card market is very dynamic. Average prices for cards decrease by roughly 40% per year as card capacities increase.

If your camera is supplied with a rechargeable lithium-ion battery it will also come with a charger. While it's usually easy to recharge the battery when you're at home, it can be worthwhile buying a spare battery so you don't run out of shooting power if you plan to travel with your camera.

Cameras that use AA or AAA batteries represent roughly half of the market and most of the lower-priced models. Some of these cameras are supplied with rechargeable AA or AAA cells and chargers but the majority come with alkaline batteries. You will save money over time by investing in at least one set of rechargeable NiMH batteries and a charger for a typical up-front cost of under A$50. Two sets of rechargeables gives you valuable back-up.

Many digicam users find the lenses on their cameras don't cover a wide enough field of view when taking pictures in small rooms or trying to capture large groups of people. Limited wide angle coverage is associated with both the small body size of compact cameras and the small size of DSC sensors, and it is rare to find a DSC with a field of view equivalent to a 28 mm lens on a 35mm camera. Some DSCs can be fitted with wide-angle accessory lenses, which will broaden the field of view but may distort the picture, producing bowed-out vertical lines. Close-up, telephoto and fish-eye adaptors are also available for some cameras.

Some cameras can be fitted with accessory lenses that extend their field of view or provide greater telephoto or close-up capabilities. These lenses are often quite heavy and they may be expensive if large areas of glass are involved.

Interesting Fact #2

Australians purchased just under one million digital cameras in 2003. Almost three quarters of them were digital still cameras, while the remainder were camcorders. Sales of DSCs more than doubled between 2002 and 2003, while camcorder sales rose by roughly 50%. The average price for both a DSC and a camcorder fell by just under 18% during the period.

In contrast, film and instant camera sales fell between 2002 and 2003, with instant camera sales roughly halved and sales of compact 35mm cameras falling by 8.2%. SLR camera sales declined by 13% and sales of compact APS cameras were almost 20% lower. However, disposable camera and 35mm film sales increased, the former by around 30% and the latter by 3%. Instant film sales fell by 19.1%.

Statistics source: GfK Marketing Services Australia

Chapter 3

How a digital image is produced

When you take a photo with a digital camera, light is focused by the camera's lens in the same way as it is in a film camera. However, instead of falling on a frame of light-sensitive film where it produces the chemical changes that allow a picture to be extracted, it falls on a silicon chip that carries a rectangular array of light-sensitive photodiodes. This 'sensor' is at the heart of all digital cameras, as shown in the illustrations below.

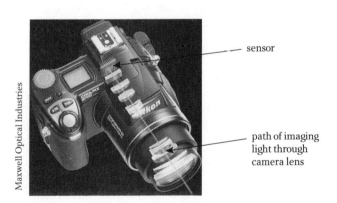

The illustration above shows the path taken by light through the lens to the image sensor at the back of the camera, where the picture information is recorded.

An enlarged view of a typical DSC sensor. The lighter grey rectangle in the centre is the photodiode array (individual photodiodes are much too small to be visible). Wires draw off the electrical signal, which is passed to the contacts ('legs') and, thereby fed into the camera's microprocessor where the image is created.

Each photodiode produces an electrical charge proportional to the amount of light it captures. However, since this only records the intensity of the incoming light, the resulting 'picture' is effectively monochrome (black and white). Colour information is obtained by covering the photodiode array with filters that separate intensity data for the red, green and blue bands of the spectrum. All colours can be produced by combining these primary colours using a process known as *colour interpolation*. The diagram on page 30 shows how it is done, while the schematic flowchart on page 1 of the colour section in this book details the processes used to convert signals that are effectively monochrome into a full colour picture.

Optical vs digital zoom

A camera's zoom lens is effectively a cropping tool that allows you to zero in on an important subject area to make it fill as much of the

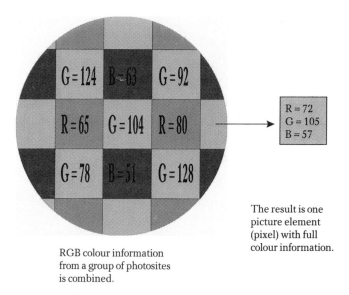

R = 72
G = 105
B = 57

The result is one
picture element
(pixel) with full
colour information.

RGB colour information
from a group of photosites
is combined.

The colour interpolation process mathematically combines the red, green and blue signal values from a cluster of filtered photodiodes (photosites) to produce individual picture elements (pixels) containing full colour and brightness information. These pixels are the basic elements of all digital photographs.

frame as you want. The lens does this optically by narrowing its view to exclude some subject areas while magnifying those that are left within the frame. When zooming optically with a digital camera, the picture area contains the full number of pixels for the selected resolution setting, but more of them are now devoted to the subject area you want, making its details clearer.

Most DSCs include a 'digital zoom' facility. This works by selecting out a rectangular area in the centre of the field of view and enlarging it to fill the frame. All 'unwanted' pixels in the surrounding area are discarded. Modern DSCs usually add new pixels on the basis of existing pixels in the selected area using a process known as 'interpolation'. Although this ensures you end up with the same number of pixels in the image, these new inter-polated pixels are created from existing image data, so you don't gain anything beyond a slightly tighter composition. The actual picture quality will depend on how many pixels your camera used to make the image and how much of that image you crop away. It will also be influenced by the quality of the camera's interpolation algorithms. High levels of digital zoom require a lot of extra pixels to be added and this usually results in a loss of both image sharpness and contrast so digital zoom shots often look much flatter and fuzzier than shots taken with the camera's optical zoom lens.

The Importance of Pixels

The term 'pixel' has been derived by combining 'picture' and 'element' and refers to the tiny blocks of colour that make up a digital image. High-quality images normally have millions of these elements and the more there are, the more detailed the picture can be and the more difficult it becomes to distinguish individual picture elements. In other words, the more 'photographic' the picture looks.

Camera manufacturers identify the resolution of DSCs by the number of picture elements the sensor can capture in 'megapixels' (millions of pixels). This megapixel count corresponds to the number of photodiodes in the sensor that are used to capture image data. While manufacturers use the term 'megapixels' to identify sensor resolution, the term 'pixels' should only be used for describing the elements in the final digital image. When describing sensor resolution, it is more appropriate to refer to the number of photodiodes or 'photosites' (the combination of photodiode plus overlying filter and microlens) that provide the data that produced the digital image. Thus a 3-megapixel camera will use data from just over three million photosites to produce an image that measures 2048 by 1536 pixels.

DSC packaging and advertising materials frequently contain two resolution figures: the 'total' number of sensor megapixels and the 'effective' megapixels. Consumers should always use the 'effective' megapixels figure when evaluating the potential resolution of a DSC because that corresponds exactly with the number of pixels in the image at the highest resolution setting. The 'total' number refers to the size of the photodiode array in the sensor, which is always more than the number of photo-sites that provide the image data. Some photodiodes are masked off to provide a reference black against which colour values are calibrated. This is their only contribution to the final image.

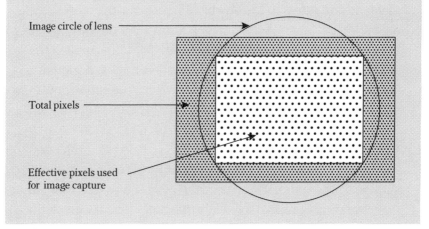

Image circle of lens

Total pixels

Effective pixels used for image capture

Sensor parameters

Few DSC buyers appreciate just how small the sensors in digital cameras actually are. In fact, it takes roughly 16 of the largest compact DSC sensors to cover a 35mm film frame and more than 30 of the sensors used in a typical 3- or 4-megapixel DSC. The situation is different for DSLR cameras, although most are roughly two-thirds the size of a 35mm film frame.

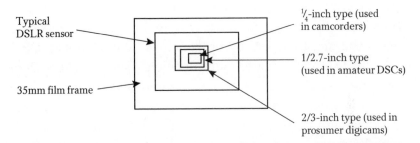

Typical DSLR sensor

35mm film frame

$\frac{1}{4}$-inch type (used in camcorders)

1/2.7-inch type (used in amateur DSCs)

2/3-inch type (used in prosumer digicams)

The diagram above shows just how much smaller a typical point-and-shoot DSC's sensor is than the sensor in a DSLR—and how much smaller both are than a 35mm film frame. Note: The 'type' designation has been inherited from the sizes used to define TV camera tubes and has a tenuous relationship with the actual size of the sensor. Originally, the measurement referred to the imaging circle of the video tube. In a digital camera, the diagonal of the sensor is roughly two thirds of the 'type' measurement.

With such small image pick-up areas, it is not surprising that the actual photodiodes are also extremely small. In a typical digicam, their surface areas range from 2.5 micrometres square to about 3.4 micrometres square. (For reference, a human hair is roughly 50 micrometres in diameter.) Such small surface areas have limited light-capturing ability, which means most DSC sensors have an inherent sensitivity similar to 50 ISO-speed film. Manufacturers increase this sensitivity by covering each photo-diode with a microlens that effectively doubles its light-capturing ability. Higher sensitivity settings are obtained by boosting the sensor signal electronically. (The resulting image noise problems are described in Chapter 9.)

Photodiodes in DSLR sensors are much larger—normally between 7.2 and 9.0 micrometres—which is at least four times the area of a digicam sensor. This means their sensitivity is higher (typically between ISO 100 and ISO 200). They are also inherently less noise prone. In many cases, this more 'normal' sensitivity to light means microlenses are not required on DSLR sensors.

Smaller sensor sizes mean that smaller lenses are required to image onto them. This, in turn, has some interesting consequences, the most important of which is that compact DSC cameras have much greater depth-of-field (see glossary) than 35mm cameras. This has both benefits and disadvantages. The more depth-of-field you have, the easier it is to ensure subjects in your photo are sharp but the more difficult it is to take portrait shots with blurred backgrounds. This topic is covered in more detail in Chapter 5.

Digital image processing

Numerous mathematical operations are required to produce every digital image and display it on the camera's monitor or store it in the camera's memory. Consequently, all DSCs need a dedicated microcomputer to carry out this processing. In most cases, the processor is an Application-Specific Integrated Circuit (or ASIC) chip or Integrated Circuit (IC) that has been designed specifically to convert the signal data that comes from the sensor into pictorial information. The efficiency and performance of the algorithms (mathematical equations) that drive the image processor can have a significant impact on picture quality and camera performance, so most manufacturers highlight the image processors when advertising new cameras.

All image processing algorithms are based on complex statistics and artificial intelligence, and they cover automatic adjustments for colour balancing, reflectance (the amount of light reflected off different elements of the subject) and lighting conditions, noise, sharpness, output dynamic range and a host of other conditions. (Output dynamic range is the range of tones between lightest and darkest in the final image which can vary according to whether the picture is printed out or viewed on a screen). New algorithms are being developed every day and continued research is leading to in-camera corrections for problems such as 'red-eye' in flash shots and lost shadow and highlight detail. A detailed understanding of image processing is not required for successful digital photography, however it's useful to know what happens when you take a digital photograph as this can help you to use your camera more effectively.

How digital photos are produced

When you press the shutter release on a DSC, a sequence of actions is initiated. By the time the button is half way down, the camera will have measured the ambient light levels and set the exposure values as well as focusing on the subject in the centre of the field of view. Pressing the button all the way down captures the image. The resulting data is stored temporarily in a buffer memory where it is sub-sampled to produce a low-resolution 'thumbnail' image that is displayed on the LCD monitor. This happens almost instantaneously, allowing the photographer to see the shot just taken.

At the same time, the signals from the sensor pass into an analogue to digital (A/D) converter, which converts them into pixel values, and then on to the ASIC digital image processor. Cameras that support continuous (or 'burst') shooting have buffer memories after the A/D converter that provide temporary storage for the digital data and will hold several unprocessed images, allowing 'bursts' of shots to be taken in quick succession. From the buffer, individual image files are fed directly into the image processor.

The main task of the image processor is to produce a full-colour picture. This is done by a colour interpolation process that takes the single-channel data from the photodiodes, which have distinct red, green or blue values, and uses them to recalculate new values so each pixel in the resulting image contains specific red, green and blue levels plus a 'brightness' value that denotes how light or dark it is. Many millions of colours can be created in this way, allowing a digital image to contain as much pictorial information as an image captured on film.

To obtain accurate colours in the resulting picture, the camera must also provide white balancing using processing algorithms that analyse the red and blue signal strengths in the image and adjust them to match the green signal strength in white and neutral areas of the picture. Further colour adjustments may also be made, usually to make the colours in the resulting picture look brighter and more vibrant, simulating the results obtained when colour films are printed.

The next image processing step involves image sharpening. Here, the algorithms work on the edges between different areas of colour and brightness to smooth and consolidate them and minimise jagged edges. Some cameras allow users to control the degree of sharpening applied to the image (a useful feature in cameras where auto sharpening is set too high for the user's taste). After this step, the processed image is ready to store on the memory card.

At this stage, the amount of data that has to be stored is very large. For example, an image from a 3-megapixel camera is about 9 MB. To increase the number of images that can be stored on the card, the microprocessor compresses the image data to reduce file sizes. Almost all DSCs use the same process for this step using the standard JPEG algorithm, an international standard that was developed by the Joint Photographic Experts Group. JPEG works by dividing the image into small blocks and discarding data in which differences are unlikely to be visible to the human eye, such as large areas of blue sky. Detailed areas receive much less data compression. Most digital cameras store JPEG images in a form specified by the Exif (Exchangeable Image File) standard. This allows the images to be opened in any software application.

Interesting Fact #3

One advantage of storing images as numbers (that is, in digital form) is that you can also store lots of associated information with the image file. The Exif standard has been developed to facilitate this process. All DSCs automatically record the following 'metadata' (data about data) for each digital photo:

- camera manufacturer and model number
- exact date and time the picture was taken
- focal length, subject distance, lens f-number and the shutter speed used to take the picture
- ambient light level, flash setting
- user-selected camera settings (sharpness level, quality level, and so forth).

The reduced-size 'thumbnail' image created when the picture is taken is stored as metadata to provide a quick low-resolution preview of the image without needing to read the entire image file. Some cameras also let users capture and store short 'sound bites' with the image as metadata, while others can store information about what the user wants to do with various images (such as the number of prints to make). With the right software application, this image metadata can simplify image retrieval and provide higher quality prints from the digital image files.

Chapter 4

The anatomy of a digital camera

A quick tour around a typical DSC will show you the location of most of the key controls and explain how they are used.

Front panel controls

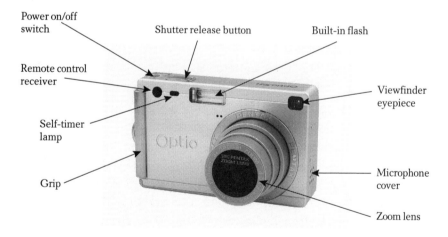

Power on/off switch

Shutter release button

Built-in flash

Remote control receiver

Viewfinder eyepiece

Self-timer lamp

Grip

Microphone cover

Zoom lens

Shutter release

The shutter determines how long the lens **aperture** remains open to let light into the camera. It's activated by a button but the actual **exposure** time is controlled automatically, according to exposure levels determined by either the camera's microprocessor or the photographer. Most cameras have a two-stage shutter button that doubles as a **focus lock**. Pressing it halfway down focuses the camera on the subject and locks the exposure and, usually, focus values. The stored settings are retained while the button is in this position, even if you move the camera. When you wish to compose shots in which the main subject is not in the centre of the field of view, just point the camera at the subject with the subject centrally located, press the shutter half way down and recompose the shot without lifting your finger. Pressing the shutter button the rest of the way down takes the photograph.

Viewfinder

The viewfinder is the 'window' you look through to compose your pictures. In most DSCs this is an optical tube that consists of a set of lenses positioned parallel to the camera's lens and linked mechanically so that when the camera's lens is zoomed, the viewfinder duplicates the action. In general, optical viewfinders show between 80% and 90% of the sensor's field of view so they cannot be relied upon for total framing accuracy, especially for close-ups, where they may show a quite different view of the subject due to the different positioning of the viewfinder and the lens that takes the picture. This phenomenon is known as 'parallax error'.

More sophisticated models have electronic viewfinders (EVF) that present the same image in the viewfinder as you see on the camera's LCD monitor, only at a reduced size. These viewfinders show you exactly what the sensor is 'seeing' as well as any shooting data that is normally displayed on the screen. However, the picture presented often looks rather grainy as the resolution of these displays is frequently quite low. Furthermore, colours may not be accurately reproduced. EVFs can also display bright vertical lines when the camera is pointed at a bright light source, which can make taking backlit shots difficult. They do not suffer from parallax error, however, and can be used for close-up shots.

Many DSCs have one or two status indicator lights positioned beside the viewfinder eyepiece. The red light normally covers flash operations and will blink while the flash is charging. In auto mode, the red light comes on if the camera will fire the flash for the shot but remains off if the flash is not required. The green light usually covers focus and/or zoom operations but may double as an indicator to show when image data is being transferred to the camera's memory card. It glows steadily when the subject is in focus but flickers when the camera is unable to focus on the subject (some cameras won't take a picture when this occurs) and blinks slowly while images are transferred to the memory card.

Flash

Most DSCs have built-in flash units that operate automatically when the camera is in auto mode and the ambient light level falls below a predetermined value. Some cameras will also activate the flash when they detect a large difference in tone between the centre of the field of view and the edges so they can even out the lighting with fill-in flash. Fill-in flash is also selectable on the majority of cameras, along with flash cancel, which prevents the flash from firing, regardless of how dark it is.

Almost all flash-equipped cameras include a red-eye reduction mode that fires one or more initial bursts of light to close down the subject's pupils so they don't photograph with red eyes. Some cameras have a night-portrait or 'slow synch' flash mode that sets the shutter speed to 1/30 second or less to ensure details in the background are recorded. In some cameras you can combine slow sync with red-eye reduction. Note: slow synch modes require the camera to be kept still while the picture is taken so when you use this mode so you should always put the camera on a tripod or steady it against a solid, stationary surface.

Lens

The lens on a DSC focuses the picture and determines how much of what you see (in other words, the angle of view you can capture) is recorded in your picture. Although some cameras (normally the smaller and/or cheaper models) have lenses with a fixed focal length, most are fitted with zoom lenses. Three times (3x) zooms are the most popular type, although DSCs with 5x, 6x, 10x and 12x zooms are also available. Most lenses carry details of the focal length limits in millimetres and the maximum apertures at each end of the optical zoom range. You can work out the zoom range by dividing the smaller focal length into the larger.

Grip

The grip can be either a moulding in the camera's body or an added bar that makes it easier to hold the camera securely. In some cases, the camera's body is enlarged (the battery compartment is often incorporated in this bulge), while in others the moulding is much more subtle. Some manufacturers apply a rubberised coating to the grip and occasionally other sections of the camera body to improve holding comfort.

Microphone

Cameras that record video clips with sound and/or voice annotations that can be attached to still shots normally have small microphones built into the camera body. Small holes in the casing show you where the microphone is located. Avoid covering these holes if you want to record sound files with your pictures as even partial blocking can cause frequencies to be lost or distorted. The same holes are used to play back recorded sounds.

Self-timer lamp

Most cameras have a self-timer that delays releasing the shutter by two or 10 seconds, allowing photographers to move into the picture. A lamp on the front of the camera indicates when the delay is activated and usually blinks faster in the last few seconds before the shot is taken. In some cameras, this lamp also doubles as a focusing aid in low light conditions.

Remote control

A few cameras can be triggered by remote control.

Rear panel controls

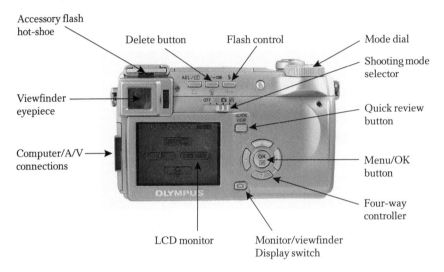

Accessory flash hot-shoe

Delete button   Flash control   Mode dial

Shooting mode selector

Viewfinder eyepiece

Quick review button

Computer/A/V connections

Menu/OK button

Four-way controller

LCD monitor   Monitor/viewfinder Display switch

LCD monitor

This viewing screen performs three main functions:

- accessing the camera's menu settings
- displaying the subject so the photographer can frame shots and check focusing
- replaying shots after they have been taken.

The screen is powered by the camera's battery so if you want to conserve power it's best to turn off the display and use the viewfinder for focusing and framing shots. (Many DSCs include a Display button for switching the monitor off and on.) Using the viewfinder can also be advantageous in bright conditions, when LCD screens can be difficult to view. Some manufacturers add an anti-reflective coating or install a reflective sheet behind the LCD to improve visibility, while a few cameras have variable angle screens that can be adjusted to improve the user's view in outdoor lighting and make it easier to use the camera for high- or low-angle shots. Neither option is a complete solution to the problem and even the new OLED (organic light-emitting diode) monitors starting to be used by some manufacturers remain difficult to use in bright conditions.

The small sizes of viewing screens can also create difficulties for camera users. Most DSC monitors have a viewing area of around 37 x 26 mm, although on cheaper cameras, 30 x 22 mm screens are common. Larger screens are usually easier to use, but they consume more power than smaller screens, which can affect the number of pictures you can take with each battery recharge. In playback mode, many cameras allow you to zoom in on pictures displayed on the monitor so you can check whether the shot is in focus (which would otherwise be difficult to do on the small screen).

Quick review button

This button provides instant playback of the last shot taken, without requiring you to switch the camera to playback mode and toggle through the menu. In most DSCs it also provides a quick way to delete shots that didn't work.

Menu

All the camera's settings are accessed via the menu button, although in some recent models, manufacturers have provided two buttons: a Function button that controls frequently used settings such as resolution/quality, ISO sensitivity, close/distant focusing, flash settings and drive/self-timer modes (different cameras have different function sets) plus a Menu button for setting controls such as white balance, noise reduction, focusing and metering modes, exposure compensation and colour, sharpness and contrast adjustments. Some cameras have separate button controls for frequently used settings such as those listed above.

The Menu button also controls all playback functions and allows camera users to change the date/time settings on the camera, format memory cards and restore all settings to the factory presets, using the 'reset defaults' control. A more detailed explanation of individual menu controls can be found in the chapters to follow.

Four-way controller

This multi-selector is used for selecting menu functions, changing camera settings and scrolling through images in playback and quick review modes. In some DSCs it may also be used to hide and display photo information on the monitor, turn the monitor on and off, or start and stop movie playback. Different cameras have different systems for many of these controls. Check your camera's instruction manual for details of how the four-way controller is used.

Delete button

Some DSCs have a dedicated Delete button that lets you erase a shot without having to access the playback menu. Pressing this button calls up the shot and gives you the option of deleting the selected shot or all the shots in the camera's memory. Think carefully before deciding to delete images because, once they have been deleted, it is extremely difficult— and often impossible—to get them back again.

Drive button

Many cameras include a dedicated Drive button that lets you select between taking one shot at a time (single shot) or a sequence of shots (continuous) when you press the shutter button. In most cameras, the number of shots you can take in a continuous 'burst' is limited by the camera's internal buffer memory. The size of the image files may also affect the number of shots per burst (although this is not always the case). A typical DSC will store between three and nine high-resolution shots in the buffer memory before it needs to process the image data and pass it to the memory card. Typical capture intervals are between one and three frames per second.

Flash button

This button controls the flash settings (see above). Users normally toggle through a sequence of preset actions and select the desired flash mode. The default setting is auto flash, which fires the flash whenever the light level falls below the point where you can easily hand-hold the camera to take a shot. Cameras that accept accessory flash units have a special hot-shoe on the top panel plus electronic controls that integrate the flash with the camera's controls to produce a correctly exposed picture.

Self-timer

This button delays the shutter release so the photographer can get into the shot. It can also be used to allow the camera to stabilise for a long time exposure. Most cameras have 10 second delays but some include two and 10 second delay settings and a few provide longer delays. In some DSCs, this button may double as a Drive or Delete button.

Computer/A/V connections

Almost all DSCs have sockets for plugging in a USB cable that allows them to be connected to a computer for downloading image files. Most also have A/V-out sockets that allow the camera to be connected to a TV set so pictures can be displayed and some have DC-in sockets that allow the camera to be powered, or the battery to be recharged, from mains power. Cameras supplied with docking 'cradles' will have most of these connections provided via the cradle.

Memory card compartment

This varies greatly among different cameras and may be located on a side panel or in the base of the camera. Some cameras have a dedicated memory card compartment, while in others it's located beside the battery, and both are accessed via the same 'door'. A few cameras include two memory card slots for different card types, giving users a choice between, say, CompactFlash and xD-Picture Cards or Memory Stick and Secure Digital cards. Not all of these cameras allow image files to be transferred from one card to another, but it's worth seeking out models that do if you have other devices that use the different card types.

Monitor/viewfinder switch
Many cameras have a switch that turns off the LCD monitor, allowing users to save power by using the viewfinder. In cameras with electronic viewfinders (EVFs), this switch toggles between the LCD and EVF.

Top panel controls

Zoom lever

Shutter button

Power switch

Mode dial

Microphone

Mode dial
Most DSCs have some kind of mode dial, which provides a quick and easy way to select key picture-taking and playback functions. Typical mode dials include between four and 10 settings and simpler cameras may only have settings for Auto, Movie, Playback and Set-up modes. The Auto setting is used for point-and-shoot photography and allows the camera to determine most picture-taking parameters. Movie mode sets the camera for video capture, while Playback is used to replay captured still or video images.

The Set-up mode is used for adjusting date/time settings, formatting cards and changing major settings (such as switching the digital zoom on and off). Details of other mode settings can be found in Chapter 5.

Zoom control

In some DSCs, the zoom lens is controlled by a rotating lever that is located in front of the shutter button, while in other cameras a rocker switch located on the back panel fulfils the same purpose. Both types of zoom control are linked to the lens and change its focal length from wide (W) to narrow (T for 'telephoto'). The zoom is used to frame shots to include things you want and exclude unwanted parts of a scene. Some cameras display an indicator in the viewfinder or on the monitor to show the amount of zoom when either button is pressed. Using the zoom control in playback mode allows you to zoom in on the displayed image to check focusing accuracy.

Downloading pictures to a PC

All DSCs are supplied with a USB cable that allows them to be connected to a personal computer and most have USB connectors that accept the smaller 'Mini B' plug. The larger USB 'A' plug fits in to the USB slot on the computer (most modern PCs have between four and six USB connections). If you're using an older operating system, you should load the driver software supplied with the camera before connecting the camera to the PC. The latest versions of Windows and Macintosh OS will recognise the camera when it's connected and activate the relevant driver.

Connecting the camera normally calls up a dialogue box that lets you choose what you want to do with the image files. In most cases it's best to click on 'Open the folder to view files' so you can see what images are stored on the card. Some software applications that are bundled with DSCs will set up albums in which you can store your pictures. These are normally labelled automatically with the date the shots were taken (or downloaded). With other cameras, you will need to set up folders on your system where images files can be stored.

It is important to decide at this stage whether you want to store your images on your PC and then return to edit them or whether you want to take your camera's memory card to a photolab to have your shots printed. In the latter case, *copying* the files to your PC produces duplicate copies of each shot but leaves the files on the camera's memory card, which can then be taken to the photolab so prints can be produced. If you *move* the files from the card to the PC, the files on the card will be deleted as they are transferred and nothing will be left on the memory card.

TV viewing

Cameras that come with A/V cables can be connected to a TV set, allowing you to view recorded pictures and video clips. The process is very simple and most cameras with this facility support both the local PAL TV standard and the NTSC standard used in Japan and North America, allowing you to view your digital photos while travelling.

Start by ensuring that the TV and camera are turned off then connect the A/V out jack on the camera to the video input terminal on the TV set using the supplied A/V cable. Turn the TV on and set it to the video input mode then switch the camera on and set it to playback and your last shot will be displayed. Playback is driven from the camera.

You can scroll through your shots by using the arrows on the camera's four-way controller and, in many cases, access the camera's playback zoom, index display and slideshow functions to show your photos on the TV screen. Conserve camera battery power by connecting the camera to mains power if available, and make sure the camera's video output signal type is the same as the TV's video signal type. (Check your instruction manuals for details.) Note: When images are compressed in order to fit the entire picture on the TV screen, a black frame may appear around the picture. If the picture is output to a video printer via the TV, this black frame may be printed. In most cases, shots taken with the panorama setting cannot be played back on a TV set.

Shots that have been taken with the camera held vertically will be displayed horizontally unless they have been re-orientated. Many cameras include either auto-rotate or manual rotating functions that let you turn such pictures 90 degrees counter-clockwise or clockwise so that they are displayed vertically. Movies, pictures taken with another camera and pictures that have been edited on a PC and downloaded to the camera's memory card cannot be rotated.

Interesting Fact #4

The LCD monitor on a digital camera uses more power than any other component in the image-recording system and if the camera has an electronic viewfinder it will also contribute to power consumption, although EVFs generally require much less power than the large LCD monitor. To extend the usable life of your camera's battery, use the viewfinder to compose shots whenever possible. However, when using the viewfinder it is important to note that the optical viewfinders in most compact DSCs show less than the picture that will be captured by the camera's sensor. A typical optical viewfinder will show between 85% and 90% of the sensor's field of view. However both LCD monitors and EVFs show the subject exactly as it is 'seen' by the sensor because the image data from the sensor is used to provide the view in each case. When shooting subjects where correct framing is critical, it is best to use the LCD monitor or EVF to compose your shot.

Chapter 5

Understanding the controls

This chapter will cover the steps necessary to take digital photographs and record video clips with a DSC. Because different cameras offer different facilities and the various controls are found in different places, these instructions are general in nature; you will need to refer to your camera's manual for precise instructions.

Before using a digital camera you must charge and install the battery, insert the memory card and set the local date and time. Once these tasks are accomplished, the camera is ready to use.

Step 1

Select the appropriate shooting mode for still pictures or video clips

In some cameras, the settings are accessed via the mode dial, while in others a slider is used to move between still and video capture modes and the playback setting. Many cameras provide several shooting modes, details of which are provided below.

Full auto ( )

In this 'point-and-shoot' mode most camera settings are controlled automatically by the camera in response to shooting conditions and the number of adjustments available to users is limited. Normally,

The different shooting mode settings on a digital camera are controlled via a mode dial, which may be located on the top or the back panel of the camera body. Turning the dial selects each mode setting.

the only adjustments you can make are to picture resolution and quality and the flash settings

Programmed auto (P)

This setting adds some degree of control overexposure metering, sensitivity, white balance and focusing. These settings are also accessible in the A, S and M modes described below. Higher-featured DSCs may also include a 'program shift' mode that can be used with the P, A and S modes to let you change aperture and shutter speed settings without altering the metered exposure level.

Aperture priority auto (A or Av)

With this setting, the photographer sets the lens aperture, while the camera adjusts the shutter speed in accordance with the ambient lighting and preset sensitivity. This mode is useful for controlling depth-of-field. For landscape shots, where you want as much of the subject as possible to be sharp, 'stopping down' to a small lens aperture (f8 to f16) is desirable, while for portrait shots 'opening' the lens to f2.8 or wider (if available) allows you to blur out distracting backgrounds. This can be difficult with compact digicams because they have between 4x and 6x the depth-of-field of 35mm cameras with the same lens focal length. In addition, most lenses can't be stopped down beyond f8. However, given

51

their extended depth-of-field, this generally produces acceptable results for landscape shots.

Shutter priority auto (S or Tv)

In shutter priority mode the photographer sets the shutter speed, while the camera determines the lens aperture to match it. This mode is handy for action shots, where high shutter speeds (1/1000 second and higher) can be used to 'freeze' the action or slow shutter speeds (1/30 second and lower) are used to blur out backgrounds in panned shots, where the photographer tracks the subject's movement with the camera and presses the shutter release when the camera is moving in synch with the subject. Shutter priority mode can also be used to select very slow shutter speeds when you want to produce misty effects with moving water.

Manual (M)

This setting gives the photographer full control over both aperture and shutter speed and often also includes manual focusing. It is used when you want full creative control over depth-of-field, exposure levels and focusing.

Many DSCs include several Scene modes, which allow photographers to preset the camera's exposure parameters for certain popular shooting situations, such as Portrait, Landscape, Sports and Night Portrait. These settings are handy for photographers who are uncertain about the best settings to use.

Portrait (🙎)

This mode applies camera settings that produce a narrow depth-of-field to isolate the subject from the background. It normally selects a large lens aperture (the maximum aperture in a compact digicam) and adjusts the shutter speed in accordance with ambient lighting. The automatic flash may fire if required, unless flash cancel has been selected. This mode is most effective when the lens is set to the 'tele' position and the subject is about 2 metres from the camera.

Landscape or Infinity (▲)

This mode sets the lens focus to near infinity and selects a small lens aperture to ensure maximum depth-of-field, ensuring that as much of the shot as possible is sharply focused. It also switches off the flash. Exact settings will depend on the ambient light level and the camera's sensitivity setting, which over-ride other settings. Use this mode whenever maximum depth-of-field is required, but not for subjects closer than 1.5–2 metres from the camera.

Sports (🏃)

This mode is used for 'freezing' action. It sets a fast shutter speed and adjusts all other parameters according to ambient light levels and camera sensitivity settings. The automatic flash will fire if required, unless flash cancel has been selected, but it may not provide adequate coverage of subjects more than 3 metres from the camera.

Close-up or Macro (🌢)

This mode is designed for taking close-ups, an area in which many DSCs excel. Some cameras can focus down to one centimetre from the lens, while others are limited to 10 cm. You can often 'bring in' more distant subjects with the zoom lens, but care must be taken with both focusing and camera stability as longer focal lengths are more difficult to focus and camera shake is amplified by image magnification.

Night Portrait (⚡SLOW or 👤*)

This mode is sometimes designated with a graphic showing a silhouetted figure plus a star or crescent moon. This mode has been set up to allow photographers to take flash shots after dark and have some background detail recorded. It combines a flash exposure that illuminates the subject with a slow shutter speed and works best when the camera is set on a tripod or steadied against a solid structure to minimise camera shake. Use the AF lock when you want off-centre subjects to be sharply focused.

Panorama

This setting—sometimes accessed via the mode dial but may be located elsewhere in the menu—helps camera users to set up a sequence of shots that can be 'stitched' together later on a PC to produce a panorama. It works by displaying a cut-down view of the last shot taken on the monitor screen. This can be used to set up the next shot in the sequence because you can see where the pictures need to be joined. Cameras that offer this mode are usually supplied with 'stitching' software. An outline of how to shoot and stitch a panorama with any digital camera (regardless of whether it provides a special shooting mode) can be found on pages 6 and 7 of the colour section, while a list of software applications that support or include panorama stitching can be found on page 175.

Additional modes

A number of digital camera manufacturers have included additional 'scene' or 'best shot' settings that set the camera's shooting parameters to match certain subject requirements. Examples include a 'Fireworks' scene that selects a very slow shutter speed, a 'Museum' scene that turns off the flash, a 'Party' scene that uses flash for all shots and a 'Beach' or 'Snow' scene that adjusts exposure levels to handle very bright conditions. Some cameras even have a 'Cuisine' scene for taking photographs of food. These settings are useful for newcomers to digital photography and can be helpful when you want to take a quick shot without toggling through a series of settings. They can also help novices to obtain better pictures. Illustrations showing the features of some of these modes can be found on page 3 in the colour insert.

The mode dials on some cameras also include positions for movie capture, playback and/or camera settings. The latter ensures that date and time settings (used to determine the correct time and date information for when the picture was taken) are recorded in the metadata that is stored with the image. They also control the file numbering system (continuous or restart each time the camera is turned on), start-up picture and sound, language, video playback format and the formatting tool that removes all files from the camera's memory. Other cameras include these functions in the general menu system. Regardless of which way these settings are accessed, they all work similarly, though some cameras provide a wider range of controls than others. More sophisticated DSCs have custom memories where users can store frequently used camera settings, allowing them to be called up with a minimum number of button presses.

Multiple-exposure modes

Many DSCs include one or more continuous shooting modes in which the camera takes a sequence of shots each time the shutter button is pressed. The most common frame rate is approximately three frames per second, although faster and slower frame rates can be found. Some cameras restrict the number of frames in a sequence due to limited buffer memory and cameras often vary in the number of shots that can be captured at different resolution settings.

A few cameras have additional (and often quite novel) multi-shot modes, such as Multishot 16, which records 16 consecutive thumbnail-sized shots and displays them as a single image (useful for motion analysis) and a 'Top/bottom' mode that records a sequence of shots but only displays and keeps the first or last four or five. Some cameras include a 'Best shot selector' (BSS) setting which captures up to 10 shots in a sequence and selects the sharpest of them for saving on the memory card. This mode is useful for situations in which inadvertent camera movement can produce blurred shots. Exposure bracketing is a variant of the BSS mode where the camera takes a series of shots, varying the exposure between one shot and the next and spanning a predetermined range. Focus bracketing, which varies the focus across a preset distance range, and white balance bracketing (which varies colour) are also available in some DSCs. In all cases, the user selects the shot that best matches the subject and discards the rest.

Step 2

Set camera resolution and quality

Better quality DSCs normally provide two image adjustment settings. The **resolution** setting determines the size of the pixel array that makes up the picture, while the **quality** setting dictates the degree to which the file has been compressed. Cameras with three quality settings usually apply the following JPEG compression ratios:

Setting	Compression ratio	When to use
Fine/high	1:4	For the best quality prints.
Normal/medium	1:8	For images that will be used in documents printed on plain office paper and smaller print sizes.
Basic/standard	1:16	For images that will be emailed or posted on web pages.

Cheaper and simpler DSCs tend to provide only one setting that covers both resolution and compression and there are variations in how different manufacturers denote the different settings, with some using 'Best', 'Better' and 'Good' for high, medium and low resolutions and others preferring 'Fine', 'Normal' and 'Standard'. You can usually judge the degree of compression by the size of the image file. A typical high-resolution/minimally compressed JPEG image from a 4-megapixel DSC is roughly 3.2 MB in size, while an image with the same resolution but the highest compression level will be just under a megabyte. An increasing number of cameras include a high-resolution/low compression 3:2 setting, which produces pictures with a 3:2 aspect ratio for printing on standard 15 x 10 cm photo paper.

A good rule of thumb is to select the highest resolution and quality settings for all shots unless you have reason to do otherwise.

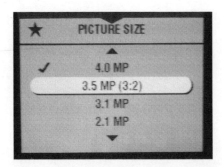

Cameras with a 3:2 setting allow users to take digital photos with the same proportions as photographs on film. This setting is ideal for images that will be printed on snapshot-sized (15 x 10 cm) paper. Note: the 3:2 aspect ratio setting is always at the highest resolution and lowest compression levels.

It is easy to reduce image file sizes without significant quality loss, should you need to do so but impossible to obtain high-quality, printable pictures from small, highly compressed image files. Some cameras include a 'small pic' button that lets you capture a small image for emailing simultaneously with a high-resolution shot, a handy feature for photographers who want both printable photos and pictures for emailing or posting on a website.

Your camera instruction manual will carry details of the different resolution and quality settings the camera supports, along with the number of pictures you can fit in the supplied memory at each setting. (Some also provide details of actual file sizes.)

Many high-resolution DSCs also support one or more uncompressed capture formats (usually TIFF and/or RAW) which capture and store every bit of data from the sensor. The size of such files is large: a typical TIFF image from a 4-megapixel camera is 12–14 MB in size, which almost fills a 16 MB card! The RAW files produced by some cameras may be compressed, but the 'lossless compression' used allows all the image data to be fully restored and the resulting files are substantially larger than the best quality JPEG files, although smaller than TIFF files. RAW files must be converted into TIFF or JPEG files before images can be viewed, edited or resized; software is provided with the camera for this purpose.

Step 3

Compose, focus and zoom

Hold the camera steady in both hands and use either the viewfinder or the LCD monitor to compose and frame the subject. Most DSCs are autofocus models, in which the camera uses a sensor (either an infrared beam or contrast detector or both) to gauge the camera-to-subject distance. Tiny internal motors then adjust the focus of the lens. Cameras without autofocusing (AF) are known as 'focus-free' or 'fixed lens' models. They work by having a small lens aperture that ensures everything between about two metres from the camera and the horizon is 'acceptably sharp'. (The 'acceptably sharp' definition is based on the premise that photos won't be printed larger than snapshot size.)

Most compact DSCs come with zoom lenses, commonly covering a 3x magnification range, although lenses with up to 12x zoom are available. The zoom is usually controlled by a lever or rocker switch, although on a few high-end digicams and all interchangeable-lens digital SLR cameras, a ring control on the lens barrel provides a much higher degree of precision and greater control. In some cameras, this ring doubles as a focus control in Manual mode.

Unlike film cameras, most DSCs include a 'digital zoom' function (in some cameras, this may be the only type of zoom available). Whereas optical zooming involves changing the lens focal length to zoom in on part of the subject, digital zoom is achieved by cropping a rectangle of pixels from the central section of the subject area and enlarging it to fill the field of view. Between 20% and 40% of the pixels are discarded in this process and, since fewer pixels are used to produce the image, some resolution is lost. Most cameras use interpolation to restore the file size to the resolution originally set by the camera user. This gives a larger file for printing, but does not produce noticeable quality improvement. Note: There is no loss of resolution with optical zoom because the lens does all the work and the resulting image contains all the pixels captured.

Before pressing the shutter release, make sure your fingers and other obstructions (such as camera straps and lens caps) are clear of the lens and flash window to ensure parts of the picture aren't blocked out. Then slowly press the shutter release all the way down to take the picture.

Step 4

Review your shot

After each shot, the picture you have just taken will be displayed briefly on the monitor before being recorded to the memory card. On some cameras you can adjust the time the shot will be displayed, but when you can't, or if you want more time to check the shot, many cameras include a quick review button that plays back the shot for as long as you require. Most cameras allow you to zoom in on the image, usually by pressing the zoom control. Some allow you to move around the displayed image by using the arrows on the four-way controller.

If you're not satisfied with the picture, you can delete the shot by pressing the delete button (which is normally indicated by a rubbish bin icon) and reshoot. This instant, on-the-spot playback is one of the most attractive features of a digital camera.

Some DSCs provide in-camera cropping facilities, which let you select part of a displayed picture and save only that portion as a separate picture. This facility can be useful when the camera's lens is not quite long enough for you to fill the field of view with the subject. It can also let you eliminate unwanted parts of a picture that you didn't notice when the shot was taken. However it's important to understand that cropping discards pixels. Crop out

When you decide to delete a digital photo, the camera usually presents you with a screen with three options: picture, exit and all. Select 'picture' to delete the image that is displayed; choose 'exit' if you have made a mistake and don't want to delete the shot and select 'all' if you want to remove all image files from the memory. Many cameras will display the message: Are you sure you want to erase this picture? If you select 'yes' the deletion will proceed. Selecting 'no' cancels the action.

40% of a picture and you lose 40% of its pixels. Consequently, it will always reduce the resolution of the image and should only be used when the size of the image after cropping is large enough for the end use of the shot.

Useful settings

Most digital cameras include an **ISO control** that lets users adjust sensor **sensitivity** levels. The default 'auto' position sets the sensor sensitivity according to ambient lighting, giving it a boost in low light levels and cutting it back in bright conditions. In most cameras, the auto range is equivalent to ISO 100 to 320. Many digital cameras offer only two or three selectable ISO settings (normally ISO 100, 200 and/or 400) but some add ISO 800 or even higher values, and a few have settings as low as ISO 50. High ISO settings should be used with great caution because they often produce shots that look very grainy and may be liberally splat-tered with white or coloured dots, which mark pixels that have not been recorded. (The issue of image 'noise' is covered in detail in Chapter 9.)

To obtain the very best picture quality, sidestep the auto ISO control and shoot at ISO 50 or 100, reserving the higher ISO settings for those times when you would be otherwise unable to take the shot. You might need to use high ISO settings when shooting action (such as sports) in dim lighting; for example at dusk or after dark with stadium lights. You need the high ISO setting so you can use fast shutter speeds to capture the action. (Use of a tripod to enable you to shoot at slow shutter speeds will normally give better results than setting a high ISO value so you can hand-hold the camera.)

Some DSCs also include in-camera **sharpness**, **contrast and saturation** controls. These are used to 'tweak' certain image parameters, either to overcome inherent problems in specific subjects or to produce results that look more attractive to the camera user. (More information on these controls can be found in Chapter 6.) In general, these adjustments are better carried out on a computer, using image editing software. When done in-camera, a limited range of adjustments is provided and it is difficult to undo adjustments that have been applied injudiciously.

Many higher-featured DSCs include a **histogram** display, a graph that shows the distribution of brightness in a photograph. The horizontal axis of the histogram represents brightness values on a scale of 0–255 (reading from left to right), while the vertical axis shows the number of pixels at each brightness level. In a correctly exposed photograph, the graph should show a relatively even distribution of pixels, peaking around the middle of the scale and tailing off towards the ends. Histograms that are weighted towards the right side of the scale indicate overexposed shots in which highlight detail is likely to be lost, while those weighted to the left show underexposed pictures (where shadow detail is compromised). Some recently released high-end digicams can provide a histogram display that evaluates the scene before you shoot, but most cameras only display a histogram in playback mode.

Most cameras come with integrated **multi-mode flash** units that provide at least three flash mode settings; normally auto flash (which fires the flash at low ambient light levels), flash off and red-eye reduction, which has been designed to prevent red eyes in flash shots of subjects looking at the camera. (The effect is due to light reflecting off the retina at the back of the eye and is worst when the pupils are wide open.) Two different strategies are used to make the pupil of the eye contract and reduce the amount of light that's reflected. Some cameras fire a series of pre-shot flashes before the actual flash shot is taken, while others shine a steady beam of light before the flash fires. Eyes react quite quickly in both cases and red-eye is usually reduced, but not totally eliminated. Fortunately, the problem can be corrected quite easily with editing software.

In March 2004, Nikon announced two DSCs with in-camera red-eye removal using an automatic red-eye detection and correction technology. All the user has to do is set the camera to the red-eye reduction mode and the recognition software does the rest. The software not only detects red eyes in images, but can also avoid false detections of potentially deceptive 'red herrings' such as polka dots and Christmas tree lights.

Some DSCs allow you to adjust the output of the built-in flash. This is advantageous as many cameras deliver a blast of light that is too powerful for many of the subjects you want to shoot (particularly close-ups and portrait shots of close subjects). Cutting the flash intensity back by a stop (or maybe more) allows you to produce shots with more natural-looking lighting. The ability to boost flash intensity can also be useful if you need to photograph large groups of people or when you want to cover a sizeable range of distances from the camera. (Be cautious about how the subject elements are arranged in your shot as close subjects may receive too much light.)

Exposure compensation and bracketing are useful tools for dealing with extreme shooting conditions, such as beach and snow scenes, backlit subjects and night shots. Most cameras offer at least two steps of overexposure to handle 'beach' and 'snow' situations and one or two steps of underexposure to adjust for low-light exposures. Because subjects can vary widely in the degree of compensation they require, photographers usually need to experiment with the exposure settings to obtain a shot in which image colours and tones are rendered naturally. This is where the instant playback facilities of a digital camera have a big advantage over a film camera.

Interesting Fact #5

The RAW setting provided on digital SLRs and DSCs designed for photo enthusiasts saves the image file with minimal post-capture processing. Photographers tend to view such files as 'digital negatives' because they can be worked upon with editing software to yield pictures that look exactly as the photographer intended. Another advantage of shooting with the RAW setting is that the large image files are transferred to the camera's memory more quickly (because minimal processing is required), which means the camera can capture a burst of shots much faster and shot-to-shot times are minimised. The downside of shooting in RAW is that special software is required to view RAW images and the images must be converted into either JPEG or TIFF format before they can be edited. Software is supplied with the camera for this purpose. Although it is possible to view RAW images on the camera they were taken with, they cannot be viewed on the screens of some portable storage devices or on TV screens and they usually need to be converted to JPEG or TIFF format before they can be printed.

Chapter 6

Controlling image colour

The white balance control is a new function found only on digital still and video cameras. It is not available when shooting with film. It's used to change the way the camera records colours so that colour reproduction is natural-looking under all types of lighting. Understanding why this control is required will help you to use it effectively and ensure the pictures you take with your digital camera or camcorder have natural-looking colours.

Why you need white balance control

The light that produces digital pictures consists of three primary colours: red, green and blue, which are the three main wavelength bands in visible light. Any colour can be produced by combining specific proportions of these three colours. This is the colour strategy used in such commonplace technologies as television sets, computer monitors and video displays. However, colours are only recorded properly when these three wavebands are in correct balance. Because our brains automatically correct global colour casts in everything we see, most people aren't even aware that in fluorescent, halogen and incandescent lighting, the ratios of the red, green and blue wavelengths are different from normal daylight. However, camera sensors will pick up these colour casts and, unless some correction is applied, the result will be photographs with unnatural-looking colours. The white balance control makes such corrections. There are examples of the colour adjustments applied by a range of typical DSC cameras on page 2 of the colour insert.

White balance is based on the ratio of the amount of blue light to the amount of red light emitted by any light source. Green is ignored as it falls in the middle of the spectrum, so its overall effect on colour balance is limited. White balance is measured in degrees Kelvin (K). A light with more blue has a higher colour temperature (higher Kelvin value) than a light with more red in it (lower Kelvin value).

The exact colour temperature of most light sources can vary due to the ageing of light bulbs or tubes, the angle of the sun, different levels of cloud and atmospheric contaminants and the colours of the subjects on which the light falls. For these reasons, most light sources are defined by a range of Kelvin values instead of one specific figure. The table on page 66 provides an overview of how the different white balance settings work.

Two factors are apparent from this table. The first is that slight colour casts are normally effectively eliminated with the auto white balance setting but strong colour casts at both ends of the spectrum require special manual compensation. The second is that fluorescent lighting is not included. This is because fluorescent lights do not emit a continuous spectrum but have discreet peaks in which one or more colours predominate. These peaks can occur at different wavelengths and, therefore, different colour adjustments will be required for different types of fluorescent lighting. Some digital cameras have several fluorescent light presets to handle these differences. It's uncommon to find labels that define which type of fluorescent light each setting matches—such as 'warm white', 'cool white' or 'daylight'—so camera users may need to experiment with several settings before they find an accurate match when fluorescent lighting is used.

Typically, three fluorescent lighting types are covered by DSCs with more than one fluorescent white balance setting:

Lighting type	Inherent colour bias (colour temperature)	Correction required	Recommended white balance setting
Clear and overcast skies at high altitudes	blue (10,000 to 15,000 K)	red	Custom/ manual
Overcast sky and open shade	pale blue (6,000 to 8,000 K)	red	Shade or cloud
Midday sunlight, clear sky	pale blue (6,500 K)	very light orange-red	Auto or sunlight
Electronic flash	pale blue (5,400 to 6,000 K)	pale orange	Auto or flash
Average sunlight	none (4800 to 5400 K)	none	Auto or sunlight
Moonlight	none (4200 K)	none	Auto
Twilight	pale red (4000K)	pale cyan	Auto
Halogen lights	pale orange (3500 K)	pale blue	Auto
100-watt light bulb	orange (2,900 K)	purplish blue	Incandescent
75-watt light bulb	orange (2,820 K)	purplish blue	Incandescent
60-watt light bulb	orange-red (2,800 K)	blue	Incandescent
40-watt light bulb	red-orange (2,650 K)	blue/cyan	Custom/ manual
Candle flame and firelight	red (1,200 to 1,500 K)	cyan	Custom/ manual

- **Bulb** represents the kind of fluorescent lighting found in domestic energy-saving lights. This is closest to incandescent lighting in colour and may be handled adequately by either the Auto or Incandescent (Tungsten) white balance setting.
- **Warm** covers the white, cool-white or warm-white fluorescent lighting that is found in standard domestic tubes. This type of

lighting can have a moderately strong green bias that may not be totally eliminated by the Fluorescent white balance setting but is usually well handled by custom ('one touch') white balance settings, which allow the actual colour of the light to be measured.

- **Daylight fluorescent** lighting is the 'coolest' of the fluorescent lighting types and may produce yellowish-green shots with the Auto white balance setting. The Fluorescent setting usually delivers better results.

White balance settings

Because all auto white balance controls work on the colours detected by a dedicated sensor, when corrections are applied, the corrections are often an approximate match to the colour temperature the sensor picks up. In most DSCs, the Auto white balance setting cannot detect colour casts beyond a fairly limited range of colour temperatures, typically between 3000 and 7000 K. Few auto settings can handle the blue casts produced by open shade or clear and overcast skies at high altitudes, or the red casts from candlelight or low-wattage incandescent lighting. In such situations, photographers should use the preset white balance modes provided by the camera manufacturer.

However, as these settings tend to use fixed values for colour temperature, if the ambient lighting does not exactly match the specified value, the correction may not be satisfactory with the colours in the resulting photographs unlikely to be reproduced correctly. Most DSC white balance settings should deliver reasonably good colour accuracy with the following lighting conditions:

- The Tungsten (Incandescent) setting corrects for lights rated at 3200 K and should work with most 80–100-watt filament lamps
- The Fluorescent setting has been designed for standard indoor fluorescent tubes and corrects for a peak green emission rated at 4000 K

- The Daylight setting is calibrated to 5500 K and is designed to match bright outdoors lighting under a blue sky—very little colour adjustment is applied
- The Flash setting matches studio flash units that emit light at 5900 K but may not be the best match for camera flash tubes
- The Cloudy setting is calibrated to 6000 K and should suit most overcast conditions. It may also work for twilight and sunset shots where the photographer wants to avoid a reddish cast in the picture.
- A few cameras include an Underwater setting that adds red filtration to compensate for the loss of the longer wavelengths, which are absorbed by water at depths below about five metres.

The white balance menu is used when you need to produce natural-looking photographs in lighting that has a different colour bias from normal daylight. Simply select the appropriate setting and the camera will adjust the colours in the shot accordingly.

Manual white balance controls

An increasing number of DSCs are being fitted with manual white balance controls. These have various names and can be referred to as 'manual', 'custom' or 'one-touch' white balance settings (or, occasionally 'preset'). The objective of all manual settings is identical: to measure the colour of the light illuminating the subject and apply the opposite coloured filtration to counteract it. The range of colour temperatures covered by the manual settings on most cameras is usually fairly wide. Most digital SLRs will span from 2000 K to 10,000 K and professional cameras can measure even higher values.

The procedure for taking a manual white balance reading is similar in most cameras:

- Switch the white balance to the manual setting.
- Place a piece of white paper, cloth or cardboard over or in front of the subject so that it is illuminated by the light source that falls on the subject.
- Point the camera at the subject and adjust its position to make the white reference sheet fill the frame. (Focus is irrelevant at this stage.)
- Press the button that sets the white balance. This stores the colour of the light in the camera, allowing the camera's micro-processor to calculate a colour balance that will counteract the captured colour bias.
- Some cameras require you to re-engage the manual white balance setting, but with most, you simply point the camera at the subject, compose the shot and take the picture. The result should be an image with natural-looking colours.

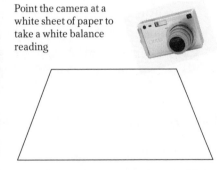

Point the camera at a white sheet of paper to take a white balance reading

Some cameras let you measure the colour of the ambient light falling on a white reference area and compensate for any colour shifts. The controls used differ from one camera to another, but in all cases, the strategy involves two steps: measuring the reference colour and applying it to the shot.

Mixed Lighting

There are times when your subject is illuminated by light sources with different colour temperatures. The most common situation is when you shoot a subject indoors under artificial lighting which is also lit by sunlight filtering in through a window. The light emitted from the indoor light bulb may be reddish while the sunlight is bluish. This mix of colour temperatures can yield interesting results but it probably won't produce accurate colours. A better solution is to use white balance control.

If you set the DSC's white balance to Auto, the camera will usually set the colour balance somewhere in the middle, making the areas lit by daylight look slightly bluish and those under indoor lighting somewhat reddish. By changing the white balance to the Tungsten setting, you can make indoor light look white and daylight look very blue. Alternatively, by selecting the Daylight setting, you can make daylight look white and indoor light very red. Another option is to use flash to illuminate the subject from the indoor side and set the white balance to either Daylight or Flash. Since both light sources have similar colour temperatures, the resulting image will be more colour-accurate, although it may lack some of the charm of the mixed lighting shot.

White balance mismatches

Colour imbalances can occur in many ways, both through measurement and human error. In Auto mode, if the white balance value is measured directly from a segment of the image containing a highly saturated single colour (such as an intense, bright red) the balance will probably be thrown off neutral, giving the resulting picture a cyan colour cast. This type of problem happens because in most cameras, the section of the field of view that is used for measuring colour values corresponds to the circle in the centre of the focusing screen. You can take a reading from a less saturated area by shifting the measuring circle to a section of the subject with a more typical mixture of colours and intensity levels, pressing the shutter release halfway down and then recomposing the shot. Pressing the shutter button the rest of the way down captures the picture.

Retention of camera settings can also create problems. Although most DSCs default to their full auto settings each time they are switched off, some retain the last settings used by the photographer. This makes it easy to shoot with the wrong white balance setting, which often produces unacceptable image colours. Because our brains quickly adjust to different colour temperatures, we are frequently unaware that a white balance mismatch has occurred until we check the shots on a computer screen and notice the colours are inaccurate. Note: relying on the camera's LCD display to check image colours is unwise because the colours displayed may not be accurate and their resolution is generally much less than the resolution of your computer screen. It is, therefore, quite difficult to assess colour accuracy on such small displays.

Digital photographers should *always* check their camera's white balance setting at the beginning of each shooting session. If you get into this habit, your chances of shooting with the incorrect setting will be minimised. Checking each shot after it has been taken will reveal gross white balance mismatches, such as the use of the incandescent light setting for shots in open shade, where the strong blue bias will be evident, and allow you to retake the shot immediately using the correct settings. Slight colour mismatches might go undetected, however.

If you have inadvertently taken shots with the wrong white balance and the difference between the correct and applied white balance settings is small, it may be possible to correct the fault with image editing software. Most applications include colour balance adjustments and, in some cases, simply clicking on the auto colour control will bring the colours back to normal. When this strategy fails, manual colour balance adjustment can be used. Unfortunately, gross mismatches, such as using the Tungsten setting under fluorescent lighting are usually impossible to correct fully unless the shot was taken in RAW format (see below).

Better software applications provide sliding controls covering the cyan to red, magenta to green and yellow to blue colour ranges. Note that these colours are complementary; moving the top (cyan/red) slider towards cyan increases the greenish-blue bias of the resulting picture. This is used to counteract a red colour cast. Moving the bottom (yellow/blue) slider to the right increases the blue bias and counteracts an excessive yellow cast. The best software packages provide separate controls over the colour balance in the shadows, midtones and highlights, allowing most slight-to-moderate colour errors to be corrected.

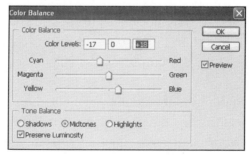

To correct an unwanted colour cast, move the sliders towards the colour that is the opposite (complementary) to the colour you wish to remove.

Photographers who shoot with the camera's RAW image setting are at an advantage when shots have been taken with incorrect white balance settings because it is easier to apply corrections when converting the RAW file to a TIFF or JPEG format. This is because the camera has done no processing of the image beyond the basic colour interpolation. When converting RAW files into TIFF or JPEG format, the software supplied with the camera allows you to adjust the colour settings as part of the conversion process. This in turn allows you to decide what changes you wish to apply to make the final picture look the way you want it to without having to process the image several times.

Saturation

Colour in digital photographs has three parameters:

1. Hue defines the wavelength of the light emitted or reflected from the image, or 'colour'.
2. Saturation defines the intensity of the hue.
3. Brightness defines the amount of hue with respect to the amount of neutral white, black or grey.

An increasing number of cameras include a setting that adjusts the **saturation levels** in the image when the photograph is taken. Normally three settings are provided: high, normal (which means no adjustment) and low. Shots taken with the setting on 'high' have more intense colours than normal. This can be particularly obvious in the red and magenta areas in a subject which take on an almost lurid glow. Shots taken with the saturation set to low can look greyish but will take on a pastel tone if the subject contains a predominance of light hues.

Some cameras also provide a **colour tone** adjustment that allows the photographer to fine tune the colour bias in shots to make skin tones look more natural. The 'high' setting in this control adds a slight yellow cast to counteract ruddy complexions, while the 'low' setting adds a reddish cast to overcome the excessive yellowish-green tones of some skin types.

Because these changes are applied as the image is captured, they are locked in and may be difficult to counteract if you find the effect unattractive when the image is opened in editing software.

As a consequence, they should be used sparingly as most such changes can be applied with much more success in editing software. If you don't like the result it is much easier to revert to the original, unaltered shot.

Digital effects include settings for capturing pictures in black and white or sepia (yellow-brown) tone to simulate old photographs. Some cameras also include a range of colour filters that change the colour of the image totally and a few include positive/negative reversal and 'posterisation' (which reduces the tonal range to produce a graphic arts effect). In most cases, these changes are best applied with image editing software as in-camera changes are not reversible.

Interesting Fact #6

Underwater photographers will be familiar with the way light is attenuated by water, with the loss of most of the reds and yellows in underwater subjects by a depth of about five metres. Digital cameras tend to be more forgiving than film cameras when it comes to colour balance but many divers and snorkellers obtain better results if they set the white balance control to the cloudy or shade preset instead of relying on the auto setting to deliver accurate colours. Use of a special 'blue water' filter (which is pinkish in hue) may provide better colour correction. Some recently released DSCs that can be used in underwater housings include an underwater setting in their white balance menus.

Colour casts in shots taken in water up to three metres deep may be difficult to detect, especially if the water is clear and the sun is high in the sky. It is usually easy to remove them by 'warming' the image slightly in image editing software. Beyond about five metres, the loss of reds in the scene is obvious and by 10–15 metres yellows are also disappearing. By 20 metres, the predominant colour is blue.

Many divers fit lights to their cameras to restore the correct colour balance so they can record all the colours of underwater subjects. In the case of DSCs, these are generally electronic flash units with a colour balance that is similar to daylight, which means the Auto and Daylight white balance settings should deliver good results. For video cameras, the lights are closer in colour to incandescent lighting and, therefore, the Indoor white balance setting should be used. However, some degree of experimentation will be required to find a setting that produces the best colour accuracy for each camera and lighting combination. Some cameras allow you to take manual readings and apply them as described above, although this may be difficult when you're 10 or more metres deep.

Exposure difficulties are also easier to overcome when shooting under water with a DSC as contrast is often much lower than it is above water. Good results can be obtained by setting the ISO value to 200 when near the surface (for snorkelling) and 400 or higher as you go deeper. Reviewing each shot after it is taken lets you check that it's what you want and reshoot if it isn't.

Chapter 7

Taking still pictures

Successful digital photography is based on correct camera usage and many potentially good pictures are ruined because people don't hold and operate their cameras correctly. Some common problems are easily identified. The classic framing problems associated with compact film cameras—cutting the tops off subjects' heads and losing the subject by concentrating on the background—can be easily prevented by checking each shot immediately. These problems are obvious when the picture is viewed so wherever possible, you should play back each shot you have taken immediately. If it's not what you want, reshoot it with the subject framed correctly. Because compact DSCs have between 4x and 10x greater depth-of-field than 35mm cameras with the same focal length, digital photographers need to pay particular attention to objects behind and beside the subjects they shoot. Shots in which trees, light poles and signs appear to 'grow' out of subjects' heads are not attractive. Check that unwanted items aren't included in the shot. It may not be possible to crop them out later without also removing some important features in the picture.

Blurred pictures are the second most common problem faced by photographers. Unfortunately camera shake, the most common reason for blurred shots, is not easy to detect on a digital camera's small viewing screen. This problem is caused by movement of the

A potentially attractive group portrait spoiled by a distracting and unattractive background.

camera during the time the shutter is open. Even a small amount of blurring can ruin an otherwise excellent picture. Some cameras will display warnings to alert you to the possibility that camera shake will occur, giving you the chance to activate the flash or increase the sensitivity (ISO) setting. Both adjustments will set a faster shutter speed to minimise the time the shutter is open. Blurring can also occur if the subject moves while the picture is

The above photographs show examples of blurring due to camera shake (left) and subject motion (right).

being taken. Blurred shots due to subject movement are easily recognised because the rest of the picture is usually sharp. Fast-moving subjects are most likely to be captured by setting fast shutter speeds or switching to the Sports scene setting.

The risk of camera shake is heightened with the use of a tele-photo lens or digital zoom as the more the subject is magnified, the more any camera movement will be magnified. Increasing the ISO setting may be the only solution because most flash units cannot provide adequate illumination beyond three or four metres and the reach of many digital zoom controls is somewhat greater.

Avoiding blurred shots

If you think you may have taken an unsharp picture, you should check the shot with the camera's playback zoom control. Most cameras allow you to magnify the image between 4x and 8x in playback mode, using the W/T zoom control and many cameras allow you to 'move' the picture around with the buttons on the four-way controller. However, if you're outdoors in bright light you may not be able to see the playback image at all and, even in indoor conditions, the screen resolution may not be good enough to reveal slight blurring. Fortunately, there are some easy strategies to prevent blurred photographs. Blurring due to subject motion can be minimised by using the Sports scene mode or setting a fast shutter speed and high ISO setting. The risk of camera shake is reduced by holding the camera and triggering the shutter correctly. Always hold the camera in both hands, making sure your fingers (and other objects) don't cover the lens or flash window. This is particularly important if the camera is small with the lens located near the edge of the camera body. If this is the case, it is easy to capture the edge of an injudiciously placed finger or the peak of the photographer's hat along one side of the shot.

Safeguard the camera by slipping the hand strap around your wrist or the neck strap around the neck. Your index finger should

The correct way to hold a compact digital still camera that has its lens located in the centre of the front panel.

The correct way to hold a digital SLR camera.

rest lightly on the shutter button, while the camera body should be supported between the remaining fingers and the thumb. Use your other hand to steady the camera. Its position may vary, depending on the size of the camera and whether the user views with the monitor or viewfinder. Take the picture by *slowly* pressing the shutter release, keeping your elbows in and holding your breath while you take the shot. Don't jerk the camera. The automatic shutter mechanism will set the correct shutter speed, no matter how quickly or slowly you press the trigger. Note: if the flash has fired, you may need to wait a second or two for the flash to recharge before taking another shot.

Tips for Successful Pictures

1. Fill the frame with the subject. Better quality results are obtained if you frame the image before you press the shutter release than by cropping the image after you've captured it.
2. Avoid shooting directly into the light unless you can keep the camera's lens in the shade. Light falling directly on the

lens will usually produce flare, which degrades image quality.

3. Mount your camera on a tripod when shooting in low light levels or with low sensitivity (ISO) settings. Use the self-timer to trigger the shutter release for long (one second or more) time exposures.

4. To avoid out-of-focus subjects in off-centre compositions, remember that the auto focus sensor in most cameras is in the middle of the frame. If you set that on the subject and half-press the shutter release before composing your shot (while keeping the shutter button down) you can lock the focus on the subject, which will be captured sharply.

5. Switch to manual focus when you're shooting subjects with very low contrast (misty scenes), very shiny objects, subjects behind glass, wire or bars and subjects moving at high speeds. Auto focus systems seldom work well in these situations.

6. Take lots of pictures. The more familiar you become with your camera, the better you will be able to use it.

(Reproduced from Digital Camera Pocket Guide, Media Publishing 2004. www.photoreview.com.au)

Viewfinder or monitor?

Photographers who use a digital SLR camera have no choice when it comes to composing their pictures as the only viewing option provided is the viewfinder. This is because the sensors used in DSLRs are of a type that does not support video capture and it is video-based technology that is used to present a 'live' view of the subject on the monitor of a compact DSC. (This is why compact DSCs can record both still pictures and video clips, while DSLRs can only capture still images.) Most compact DSC owners find it easiest to frame shots by viewing subjects with the LCD monitor. All that's required is to point the camera at the subject and press the shutter. If you've done this correctly, the image you see when the shot is played back should match the picture you composed. However, there are times when using the viewfinder is a better option. LCDs are universally difficult to view in bright outdoor lighting. Some camera manufacturers provide clip-on screens to shield the screen from direct light but these are only partially successful at best. For most outdoor shots in bright sunlight, use of the viewfinder is the only way of seeing the subject well enough to compose your shot satisfactorily. Note: the viewfinder also uses less power than the LCD monitor so, if your camera's battery indicator is low, switching the display off and using the viewfinder will allow you to continue taking pictures for a while longer. Unfortunately, many people find optical viewfinders difficult to use. If your snapshot collection contains numerous shots in which the tops of people's heads are 'cut off' or trees and posts appear to 'grow' out of people's heads, you could have this problem. You can train yourself to use a viewfinder effectively by checking what is and is not included in each shot before you press the shutter button. Have you filled the frame with the subject? Does the main subject look sharp? Is there anything else in the frame, such as a tree or distracting area of light, that spoils the shot? If you go through these checks deliberately before taking each shot, then check the result immediately, you will soon learn what does and doesn't work. In time, the process will become automatic and you will carry out the preshooting check automatically. However, the optical viewfinders on most DSCs do have some limitations:

1. Few of them cover exactly the same field of view as the sensor 'sees'. In most cases, coverage ranges from about 75% to 95%.

The above pictures show how much discrepancy there can be between what the optical viewfinder in a camera 'sees' (left) and the picture recorded by the camera's sensor (right). The differences may not be significant in snapshots but are important in situations where accurate framing is critical.

2. The optical viewfinder on a compact camera never shows the correct view of the subject in a close-up shot. They don't 'see' it as the camera's lens does because the viewfinder's window is in a different place from the camera's lens. This positional difference causes no apparent problems with subjects that are more than a metre or so from the camera but becomes very obvious with close subjects. The effect is known as 'parallax error' and the only way to overcome it is to frame all close-up shots by using the LCD monitor.

The above pictures show the difference between what the optical viewfinder sees for a typical close-up shot (left) and what the monitor displays and the sensor captures (right).

Digicams with electronic viewfinders (EVFs) use the signals from the camera's sensor and, unlike optical viewfinders, will provide an accurate view of the subject the sensor captures. This means they are reliable for close-up shots. EVFs have a second advantage in that they can display the same information you normally see on the LCD screen. This is particularly useful when the camera has a large number of user-adjustable settings because you can change settings and see the changes without having to look away from the subject. For this reason, the majority of 'prosumer' digicams are fitted with EVFs. However, EVFs have some inherent problems that can affect their usability. Because they rely on normal LCD technology, their resolution is often low and the view of the subject may be 'grainy'. Colours may not be accurately reproduced and white streaks may cross the field of view when the camera is pointed at brightly lit subjects (especially where there are specular reflections off shiny surfaces like chrome and glass). These streaks also appear on the LCD monitor so they can't be avoided by switching from viewfinder to monitor. They can make it difficult to compose a picture but, fortunately, rarely affect the image that is captured by the sensor itself. The sensor has much higher resolution and the camera's processing system will usually eliminate all but the grossest defects. Digital SLR cameras do not suffer from parallax error and, because the same lens is used for viewing the subject and taking the picture, they generally record everything the photographer sees.

Auto or manual focusing?

Compact DSCs come with either of two focusing options: fixed focus (also known as 'focus free'), and auto focusing. In a fixed-focus camera, the focus is non-adjustable and the camera has a small lens aperture to provide an extended depth-of-field. These are more common among the lower-priced models and can only be used for shooting subjects that are more than one metre from the camera. Anything closer will be out of focus. The majority of DSCs are auto focus (AF) models. This option suits most users and the commonly used auto focus DSCs work well in most situations. Four types are in common use:

1. Infrared ('active') AF fires a beam of infrared light at the subject and measures the time it takes for the reflection to return. The subject distance is set on this basis. One advantage of this type of system is that it works in the dark, which means you can take low-light shots with flash and expect them to be in focus.
2. Contrast-based ('passive') AF, which evaluates the overall contrast in a scene and sets the focus to ensure those areas with the highest contrast (which normally represent the main subject) are sharp. These systems require light to operate so cameras with passive AF systems require a built-in AF illuminator light to give the AF system some information to work with in dim lighting.
3. Video AF systems are a variant of contrast-based AF systems in which the camera's image processor evaluates the signal intensity differences between adjacent strips of photodiodes and drives the lens back and forth to find the point where they are at a maximum. They also require adequate lighting to focus correctly.
4. Hybrid systems combine infrared with passive focus detection and swap between them according to the type of subject the photographer is capturing.

SLR cameras with interchangeable lenses normally use contrast-based AF systems, while point-and-shoot DSCs may have infrared or contrast-based AF controls and some have hybrid systems. Some higher-featured DSCs use video AF. If the specifications in your camera's instruction manual don't show what type of focusing your camera has, you can determine whether it's active or passive with this simple test. Take the camera outdoors and, using the viewfinder, aim it at an area of clear sky with no clouds, power

Turning numbers into pictures: how a digital colour photo is created

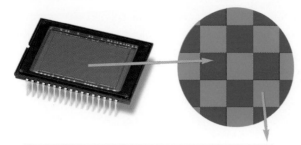

Each photosite in the sensor collects a light value for either red, green or blue.

Colour interpolation combines these values to produce individual pixels with different proportions of red, green and blue, resulting in a full colour photographic image.

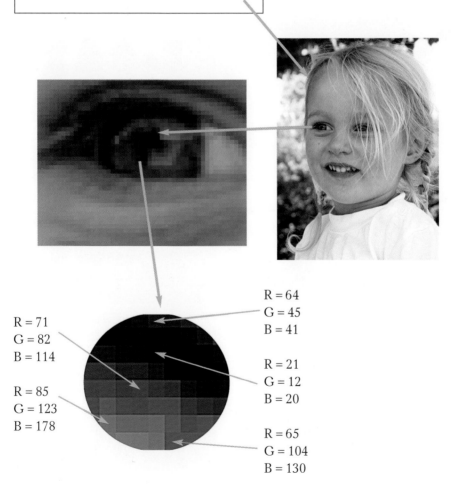

R = 64
G = 45
B = 41

R = 71
G = 82
B = 114

R = 21
G = 12
B = 20

R = 85
G = 123
B = 178

R = 65
G = 104
B = 130

How the white balance control works

The white balance control uses colour filtration to counteract the colour casts introduced by different types of lighting. The examples below show the colour and the degree of colour compensation provided by the most common white balance settings on digital cameras.

Normal subject colours

Daylight (very slight warming)

Cloudy (visible warming)

Flash (warm yellow bias)

Fluorescent lighting (magenta and blue to counteract excess green)

Incandescent lighting (strong blue to counteract excess red)

Shade (moderate warming)

Using scene menus

The illustrations on this page show some of the options available via the Scene menus in some DSCs. They have been taken mainly from Casio cameras (which have the broadest range) but other brands also provide similar on-screen illustrations to help camera users.

Colour controls in photo editing software

1. Colour ring-around

Ring-around controls present you with a 'ring' of thumbnail images surrounding your central selected image or lined up below it. Each thumbnail in the ring shows a different colour variation. You simply select the one that best matches the desired end result and click on it to apply the change. The illustration below shows the Photoshop Elements 3.0 colour ring-around, which is accessed by clicking Enhance>Adjust Colour> ColorVariations.

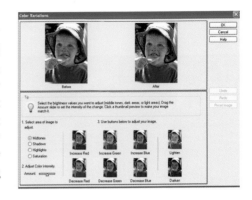

2. Eyedropper systems let you set a 'neutral grey' point by clicking on an eyedropper icon and positioning it on an area in the image that should be white, black or grey. All image colours will then be adjusted to be in balance with that neutral reference and should, in theory at least, be correct.

3. Slider controls normally cover three adjustments: Hue, Saturation and Lightness. The hue control adjusts the colour, the saturation, the intensity of the hue and the lightness ranges from black on the left to white on the right of the scale. Each slider covers a very broad range of adjustments, as shown in the sample images from the lower and upper extremes of the saturation scale. As a result, care is required when changing any setting.

Low saturation

High saturation

4

How to correct red eyes in flash shots

Red eyes are quite common in portrait shots taken with on-camera flash units and often ruin otherwise excellent shots. The problem is easy to correct and many software applications have special tools for that very purpose. However, some work better than others, so it's handy to know how to do the job from scratch.

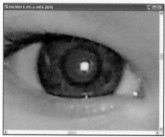

1. Start by enlarging the section of the picture containing one of the red eyes.

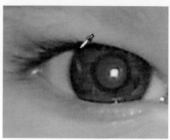

2. Using the eyedropper tool, sample the darkest area of the eye to obtain a colour for 'painting out' the red.

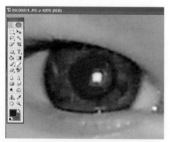

3. Then, using the pencil or brush tool, 'paint' over the red areas, leaving the white catch-lights untouched.

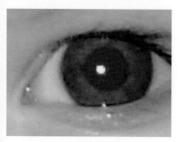

4. Repeat with the other eye.

The result

Produce a perfect panorama

First capture the scene.

1. Decide where the picture will start and end and stand in a position that will let you cover the entire scene without having to move.

2. Working from left to right, take a sequence of shots, overlapping adjacent pictures by at least 30%. If your camera provides a framing guide in the viewfinder use it, but note that when you're shooting in bright outdoor lighting, this guide may be unusable and you'll have to rely on guesswork to frame the shots. Keep your feet in the same position and swivel from your hips as you pan across the scene. Don't change any of the camera settings between shots and try to capture all the shots as quickly as possible.

Then create the panorama.

Download your panorama shots to your computer then load the panorama stitching software. In most cases, the software will provide adequate guidance.

1. Load the images into the software application in order.

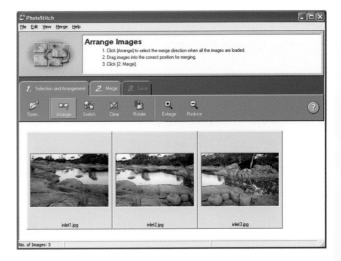

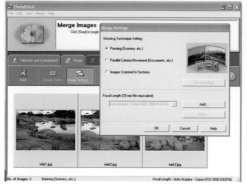

2. Check the stitch settings to ensure you are using the correct parameters then click on the 'stitch' or 'merge' button. The software should assemble all the images to create the panorama.

3. Enlarge the result to ensure the images are correctly sequenced and joined at the right places. Most applications provide a cropping tool that lets you trim off the 'ragged' edges. Then save the image. Don't worry if there are minor imperfections at this stage as you will fix them in step 4.

4. Open the panorama in your favourite editing application and use the cloning tool to smooth over minor discontinuities in the merged image. Always work on an enlarged copy of the image so you can see exactly what you're doing. Resave the final result.

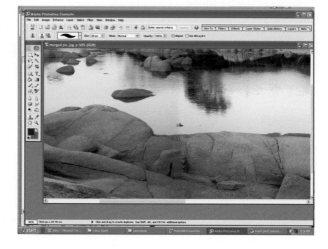

Inkjet printing problems

There is no longer any doubt that inkjet printers can produce prints that are as good as—and in some cases better than—prints from conventional photographs. However, some problems can occur when the prints are displayed. Similar problems also occur when prints from the photolab are displayed but inkjet prints often react quite differently from photo prints and, if you can identify problems in the early stages, it may be possible to arrest fading and colour changes before they become noticeable—or even prevent them from occurring altogether.

The illustrations on this page show some typical examples of how fading and chemical changes can affect inkjet prints. In each case, the original camera image is shown for comparison.

1. Fading
Fading can affect all colours globally, leaving a washed-out appearance or it can reduce some colours more than others. The example below shows the effects of global fading on a print that was displayed in normal room lighting for eight months.

The original picture

After 8 months on display

2. Colour changes
The most common colour change is the loss of all blue hues, leaving the picture with a strong orange cast. The next hue to disappear is green, making the picture appear reddish. The example below shows how colour change has affected a print that was kept in a drawer for eight months.

The original image

Discolouration produced after 8 months

3. When fading and colour changes combine, the result can be quite dramatic and the print is generally unusable. The example below shows a print that has been left in a room with computer equipment, where it received approximately 30 minutes of direct sunlight each day.

The original image

Fading and discolouration resulting from exposure to direct sunlight and environmental contaminants.

lines or tree limbs. Press the shutter button halfway down. If the focus indicator beside the viewfinder eyepiece shows the shot is in focus, it's an active AF system. If you get an out-of-focus indication, it's a passive AF system (the sensor can't find any contrast in a blue sky, so it gives up). Cameras with hybrid AF systems will switch to infrared evaluation and indicate correct focus.

Using auto focus effectively

In most cases, the AF control on a DSC should lock onto the subject in less than half a second, which is as fast as your eye can change focus. However, there are some subjects that will cause the AF system to 'hunt' backwards and forwards in an effort to find something to focus on. The delay that occurs during this hunting process is known as 'auto focus lag'.

Cameras with infrared AF systems can find it difficult to focus on distant subjects because the infrared beam doesn't reach much beyond 8–10 metres. They can also produce out-of-focus shots when the subject is behind a pane of glass, wire mesh or bars because the AF system will focus on the closest surface (the glass, wire or bars). Cameras with contrast-based and video AF systems have difficulty focusing in low-contrast situations, such as mist or fog, and with subjects that have little or no detail, such as large areas of one colour.

Problem subjects for auto focusing systems:

Subjects behind wire, bars or glass (the camera will focus on the nearest object).

Low-contrast subjects

Fast-moving subjects in dim lighting.

Many recently released cameras automatically switch to infinity focus when their AF sensor cannot focus, on the assumption that the subject is further than about 10 metres from the camera. This focuses the lens on the background, which may not be what is required. Most AF cameras include a focus lock setting, which lets the photographer choose an area within the subject to focus on and then recompose the shot so this area will be sharp in the picture. The process is simple and effective.

1. Compose the picture so the focus sensor in the centre of the field of view is positioned over the main subject.
2. Press the shutter release halfway down and hold it there. This locks the focus and exposure on the main subject.
3. Keeping the shutter release half-pressed, recompose the shot. You can shift the camera to place the main subject at either side of the picture without changing either the focus or exposure as long as the shutter button remains half way down.
4. When you are happy with your composition, press the shutter button the rest of the way down to take the shot.

How to use the focus lock: centre the focus sensor on the subject (left) then press the shutter release half way down and recompose the shot (right).

Using manual focus

Many DSCs provide a manual focus setting that can be used when the AF system fails to focus quickly enough. In some cameras, a series of preset focus distances is provided, while DSLR cameras and some prosumer digicams have manual focus rings. To use the distance scale, you must estimate the camera-to-subject distance then select the manual focus setting in the camera's menu system using the four-way controller. With most compact digicams, setting a precise focusing distance is unnecessary because the depth-of-field provided by these cameras is normally more than enough to span the difference between one distance setting and the next. Near enough is usually good enough. Focusing rings provide a much more accurate way to focus precisely, which is why they are used in the types of cameras that attract serious photographers.

Auto or manual exposure?

All DSCs measure and set exposure values automatically but many provide users with a number of auto exposure (AE) options, which cover both the way exposure is measured and the extent to which the actual exposure can be made to vary from the metered value. Three AE metering patterns are in common use: multi-pattern (variants of which include 'matrix' and 'evaluative' metering), centre-weighted average metering and spot (or partial) metering.

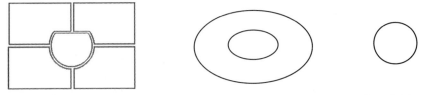

The three most common metering patterns used in digital cameras (from left): multi-pattern, centre-weighted and spot.

Multi-pattern metering systems split the subject into a matrix of discrete areas, in which individual brightness levels are measured separately. The brightness measurements are fed into the camera's microprocessor where algorithms calculate an averaged exposure setting. The number of metering zones ranges from five to over 350 and each manufacturer has developed its own set of algorithms that apply certain biases to values from different parts of the field of view. For example, greater weighting is usually placed on the central and lower areas in landscape shots. Multi-pattern metering systems usually deliver the best exposure settings for most snapshots and also work well for a wide range of subject types.

Centre-weighted average metering systems average the brightness values over the entire field of view but give greater weight to values from the central area. These systems work well for centrally placed subjects but may produce underexposed photos with landscape shots that have large areas of sky.

Spot and partial metering systems differ only in the size of the metering area. Spot metering areas range from 3% to 8% of the field of view, while partial metering area covers between 8 and 12%. Brightness values are obtained only from the selected area so these systems provide the most accurate readings when correct exposure for a specific area in the subject is required. You can use spot metering with the AF/AE lock (by half-pressing the shutter button) to measure selected areas in the camera's field of view. This lets you identify both the brightest and darkest areas in the shot and determine the dynamic range in the subject.

There are times when the AE system does not deliver a correctly exposed photograph, the most common being in the very bright conditions you find on the beach or ski slopes. In such cases, the picture will be underexposed because all AE systems work by averaging the brightness values. The reverse occurs when very bright subjects are positioned against a dark background, a common situation with theatrical performances. In both cases, the photographer must take control and adjust the exposure using the exposure compensation setting.

Problem subjects for auto exposure systems:

Very bright scenes, such as beaches or snowfields.

Light subjects against very dark backgrounds.

Subjects with unequal amounts of light and dark tones.

Most cameras include at least two f-stops of exposure compensation, normally over- and underexposure. Although it may seem counterintuitive, in order to obtain the most natural tonal values for shots taken in bright conditions, set the exposure compensation to +1–2 EV (exposure values, which are the equivalent of f-stops). Shots taken in low lighting will usually require between 0.5 and 2.0 EV of underexposure (-EV) to match the tonal values to those in the original subject.

Flash or available lighting?

Like photographers who shoot on film, digital photographers can choose between taking pictures with available lighting or flash as most DSCs are fitted with built-in flash units. In many outdoor situations, use of the flash is unnecessary. However, there are times when boosting available light levels with the flash will yield better pictures. The most common of these is for backlit shots, particularly portraits, where the light comes from behind the subject. In such situations, unless spot metering is used, the subject's face will be underexposed and appear quite dark. Using a 'fill-in' flash illuminates the shadowed area, bringing a more natural-looking balance to the shot.

Subjects that are lit from behind or have shaded faces from wearing hats can be improved by using fill-in flash to illuminate the shadowed areas.

The default flash setting for DSCs is auto flash, which means the flash will be activated whenever ambient light levels fall below a predetermined value. In most situations, the auto setting will produce acceptable results, but success is by no means universal. Close-ups are often overexposed by flash shots, while subjects beyond three metres are commonly underexposed, especially if there is a large expanse of dark behind them. Some cameras provide flash compensation to deal with these situations. This works in a similar way to exposure compensation but adjusts flash output instead of exposure levels. However, it is more common to be offered a 'slow synch' or 'night portrait' setting, which selects a slow shutter speed (and may also reduce the flash output slightly) to provide a better balance between the flash and the ambient lighting in portraits taken after dark. It is normal for cameras to use shutter speeds of between one half and 1/30 of a second for such exposures. Consequently, there is a high risk of camera shake. When using slow synch or night portrait modes, make sure the camera is kept steady while the shutter remains open. Either mount the camera on a tripod or stabilise it against a wall or other solid, non-moving object before pressing the shutter release and keep it still until the shot is displayed on the LCD screen.

The picture on the left was taken with the standard auto flash setting, while the one on the right was taken with slow synch flash. Note how much more background detail is recorded with the slow synch setting.

Taking pictures in a hurry

When you're taking photos of children playing, sporting events, parties or special ceremonies, fiddling with camera controls and checking each shot after taking it can cause you to miss some great pictures. All photographers know that the more shots you take, the better your chance of capturing a truly memorable image. Digital cameras provide an easy and comparatively cheap way to take plenty of shots.

1. Start with a large memory card—at least 256 MB. This allows you to record several films' worth of photos.

2. Set the camera to the auto or 'P' mode so it will adjust exposure values automatically.

3. Use the burst or 'best shot' continuous capture mode to take three or four frames in rapid succession when taking action shots. It's often the only way to ensure you capture the critical point in the action, allowing you to select the best shot and discard the remainder.

4. Prefocus wherever possible to eliminate focus lag. If the subject is moving towards you, estimate the distance at which it will fill the frame and press the shutter halfway down (or preset the distance if your camera permits) to lock the focus. When the subject reaches that point, press the shutter button all the way down to capture the shot.

5. Use the camera's highest resolution and quality settings. This may sound counterintuitive but the less processing the camera's internal computer has to do, the faster it can send data to the memory card.

6. Start with fully charged batteries and compose shots with the viewfinder rather than the monitor. The more power the camera's microprocessor can access, the more efficient it will be.

7. Use the 'quick view' function on your camera, rather than the playback setting for checking shots. It's quicker because pressing the shutter button resets the camera to capture mode with minimal delay.

8. Only review shots when there's a definite break in the action or if you need to free up space on the memory card. This is the time to delete the obvious dud shots (but not 'borderline' duds). Make sure you reset the camera to shooting mode when you've finished.

Continuous shooting

Some cameras support several continuous shooting modes (see Chapter 5). The most common 'burst' mode involves capturing a sequence of shots in quick succession at intervals that may vary from less than half a second to around one second. The shot rate may vary with the chosen image size and the number of shots is usually determined by the size of the internal 'buffer' memory in the camera, so shot resolution can determine the number of shots in a burst. However, some cameras can keep shooting in burst mode until the memory card is full, although their capture rate may be quite slow. An increasing number of cameras come with multishot burst settings, which can capture a sequence of shots (normally 16) in rapid succession when the shutter button is pressed. The shots are saved together as a single file and, when displayed or printed, each individual picture is thumbnail-sized. It is common to offer two multishot modes: one which captures 16 shots when the shutter is pressed and saves the result, and another which starts recording shots when the shutter is pressed but only records the last 16 in the sequence. A few cameras allow users to adjust the intervals at which shots are recorded in these modes but with most, the user is stuck with the manufacturer's settings. Multishot capture has a number of handy applications. Some photographers use the sequential capture ('normal' bust) mode to overcome shutter lag—although this is much less of a problem with the latest DSCs than it was with cameras released before mid 2003. Others use it for motion analysis, particularly for sports such as golf (for documenting club swings), cricket and baseball (pitching, bowling and batting actions), gymnastics, diving and dance. The 'last burst' multishot 16 mode is useful for recording anticipated actions that may peak unpredictably, such as the blowing out of candles. The photographer presses the shutter when the action is anticipated and only releases it when the action has been completed, knowing that the 16 shots will have captured the action's peak. Note: images captured in multishot mode are generally small with low resolution as typical file sizes are less that 2 MB for a file containing 16 shots.

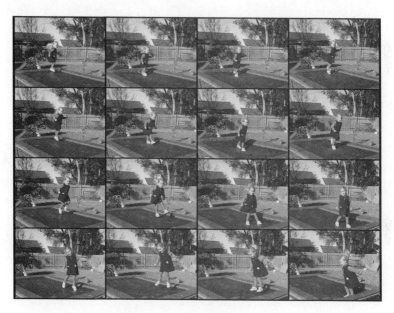

A typical multishot image file.

Overcoming shutter and AF lag

It is rare to find any camera—film or digital—that can lock onto a subject and capture an image instantaneously. There is always some lag between when the shutter button is pressed and when the picture is captured although, with some subjects (and some cameras) this lag is small enough to be undetectable by the photographer. The most common source of lag is the time required for the AF system to lock onto the subject, which can extend to more than one second with the problems described earlier in this chapter. Until recently, shutter lag was a serious problem with DSCs, with delays of one second or more being relatively common. However a shutter lag greater than 0.5 seconds is now quite rare.

Nevertheless, when a 0.5 second shutter lag is combined with an AF lag of 0.5 seconds or more, the resulting delay can reduce the photographer's chance of capturing the 'critical moment' in a shot. Because they are so closely linked, shutter lag and AF lag must be tackled together and there are several strategies that work reasonably well, although not necessarily in all situations.

1. Prefocus the camera on the subject. This can cut lag times to less than 0.2 seconds, which is almost undetectable. However, the strategy will only work when you know where the subject is going to be when the shutter is released. Some cameras have focus tracking settings that readjust the focus continuously, regardless of how the subject is moving. Others include a 'predictive' AF control that measures the position, speed and direction of the subject's motion and estimates where it will be when the shutter is pressed. These systems are usually effective but they tend to be quite power-hungry and will reduce the effective life of the camera's battery.

2. Set the camera to burst mode. This minimises delays between shots and it is usually possible to obtain one shot from the sequence in which the subject is sharp. Some cameras automate this process under the tag 'Best shot selector', while others include slight focus adjustments between one shot and the next to cover anticipated movement. Shutter lag alone can be minimised by reducing the amount of processing the camera's microprocessor has to do and maximising the amount of power available to the microprocessor. Turn off the LCD display and shoot at the highest resolution and quality setting, avoiding post-capture processing like sharpness, contrast and saturation adjustments (which are best done with editing software). Keep batteries fully charged wherever possible.

Interesting Fact #7

Light intensity diminishes with distance. While an object that is one metre from a light source may receive an adequate amount of light, if you move it to two metres away it will receive half the light intensity. Moving it to within half a metre of the light will double the intensity it receives. This rule also applies flash exposures. The working range of most built-in flash units is between 50 cm and two metres. Subjects closer than 50 cm are likely to be overexposed, while those beyond three meters will not receive enough light to capture details, and by the time they are four metres away, the amount of light they receive is negligible.

Note: when shooting scenic shots such as cityscapes outdoors, set the flash to 'off' to ensure the exposure is long enough to record the details you want to capture. Use of a tripod is advisable for exposures longer than 1/30 of a second.

Chapter 8

Movie capture

If you want a camera that can capture digital video clips, there are two choices available. You can opt for a digital camcorder which has been designed specifically for that purpose, or select a compact DSC with video recording capabilities. However, the situation is not quite as straightforward as it might seem. Because digital camcorders have been purpose-designed for video capture, their controls have been optimised for shooting videos, which is quite different from taking still pictures. There are also pros and cons in the design parameters that camera users must consider when choosing whether to take videos with a camcorder or a DSC.

Most camcorders have longer zoom lenses than DSCs because they are used to cover a much wider range of subject distances. Because we view video at much lower resolution than still images, camcorder lenses are often smaller and may be less technologically sophisticated than DSC lenses. This is not always the case, though, as most cheaper DSCs have inexpensive, simple optics while the highest-priced camcorders have high-quality, technologically complex optics.

Camcorder sensors are generally smaller than compact DSC sensors because their main purpose is to produce video. Few TV screens can display more than 500–600 lines so, unless the camcorder also supports still image capture, there is no reason to provide a resolution higher than 0.8 megapixels. Camcorders that capture both still and video pictures have higher sensor resolutions but they use the sensor differently for each function. When a high-resolution still picture is recorded, the full effective sensor area is utilised, but when video is captured, only part of the array is used. For standard 4:3 format video, it's the central portion of the sensor array, while for 16:9 'widescreen' video, data is captured from a central rectangle with the same aspect ratio (data from the upper and lower sections of the array is ignored).

Camcorders record image data onto videotape or a DVD, both of which provide plenty of storage space very cost-effectively. They also capture audio along with video images and devote a substantial part of their data processing to this purpose. Consequently it is unlikely that pictures from video camcorders will match the resolution of a fairly average DSC. It simply isn't necessary. This situation may change when high-definition television is introduced, but it won't change much.

The video capture capabilities of a DSC have evolved from the need to provide a live display on a small screen and, consequently, all compact DSCs can record video, although not necessarily with sound. However, most DSCs can only capture video at comparatively low resolution and their frame rates seldom match the rate of 25 frames per second of dedicated video camcorders. As a result, video from DSCs is often jerky and the size of the display may be quite small. Recently, some manufacturers have introduced improved video capture facilities in their higher-featured DSC models and some of these come close to matching the video clips produced by digital camcorders. Frame rates of 30 frames per second are becoming more common, reducing the jerkiness of earlier models. More DSCs are starting to offer VGA (640 x 480 pixel) video with sound, although the sound is usually monaural (whereas camcorders generally capture stereo sound).

One problem yet to be solved concerns storage of video clips captured on a DSC because even low-resolution clips use up a lot of megabytes. As a consequence, DSC manufacturers often limit the length of the movie clips to a few seconds to avoid overloading the buffer memory. Many also use very high compression ratios for video clips, simply to optimise the amount of video that can be captured and stored. This can result in video quality that is noticeably lower than video captured on tape or optical disk, regardless of the resolution and frame rate. The table below indicates how much video you can store at the various resolutions and frame rates supported by DSCs. The figures provided are for video clips with sound; silent video files are slightly smaller.

Media capacity	Resolution and frame rate (frames per second/fps)		
	640 x 480 30 fps	320 x 240 15 fps	160 x 120 15 fps
16 MB	Approx. 12 sec.	Approx. 45 sec	Approx. 100 sec
32 MB	Approx. 25 sec	Approx. 105 sec	Approx. 3.5 min
64 MB	Approx. 55 sec	Approx. 3.5 min	Approx. 7.2 min
128 MB	Approx. 120 sec	Approx. 6.0 min	Approx. 14.4 min

Source: Advanced Digital Photography, Media Publishing, 2004.
www.photoreview.com.au

Given these figures, we are unlikely to see a DSC that can capture and store video as cost-effectively as a digital camcorder in the foreseeable future. However, with the current technology convergence, the still picture capture of camcorders is improving. During 2003, the first camcorders with 3-megapixel sensors were released and all had separate memory card slots for still image storage. In use, these camcorders captured still shots at the full resolution of the sensor, producing images files of 1152 x 864 pixels. However they reduced the effective resolution to 690,000 pixels for video to match standard display requirements.

The memory card market is also evolving rapidly. Card capacities have doubled in most card types over the past 12 months and prices have fallen by between 30% and 40% each year. The table in Appendix 1 compares prices and card capacities as they were in late 2004. Updates to this table will be provided at www.photoreview.com.au as significant price changes occur. Once high-capacity memory cards are cost-competitive with videotape and once consumers have facilities for storing the vast amounts of data involved in high-resolution video capture, we will probably see a move from tape-based video to solid state, card-based storage. But don't hold your breath. The cheapest price we could find for a 1 GB memory card, which can hold 16 minutes of VGA video at 30 fps, was around A$300. With a 30-minute MiniDV tape costing around A$10, the playing field is still somewhat less than level.

DVD camcorders could provide a bridging solution because the 8 cm disks they use can hold 1.4 GB of data. But when we went to press the highest sensor resolution was only 2-megapixels, which is suitable only for snapshot-sized prints.

The basic message to consumers who want to shoot video is simple: you need to decide on your priorities. If video is more important than still capture, buy a digital camcorder; if still capture is more important than video, buy a DSC. If you want both, be prepared to compromise on one of the two functions.

Digital Camera Choices

Function	Digital still camera	Digital camcorder
Still picture resolution	Higher (up to 8 megapixels)	Lower (0.8–3 megapixels)
Available still file formats	JPEG, TIFF, RAW	JPEG only
White balance presets	Many (5–8 plus manual)	Few (2–3 plus manual)
Video resolution	VGA, QVGA, QQVGA*	VGA
Video frame rate	12–30 fps	25 fps
Audio/sound	Monaural	PCM Stereo
Media cost vs capacity	High (cards)	Low (tape or disk)

*VGA = 640 x 480 pixels, QVGA = 320 x 240 pixels, QQVGA = 160 x 120 pixels.

Choosing a still camera for video

If you want a DSC with both still and video capabilities, cross digital SLR cameras off your list. No DSLR can capture video clips or display a live view of the subject because the sensors used for cameras of this type record information all at once (in the same way as film records a single frame), whereas digicam sensors capture data using a scanning process that allows a moving image to be displayed. Compact digicams with video capabilities vary greatly in both the quality of their video, the permitted clip lengths and their audio capture capabilities.

Some compact digicams have been designed to capture video clips with sound at VGA resolution with a frame rate of 30 frames per second.

When you use a DSC to capture video, the resolution setting determines the size at which the resulting video will appear on a computer screen and whether the quality of the video is good enough to play back on a normal television set. Video clips captured at VGA resolution (640 x 480 pixels) are usually good enough for TV playback (especially if frame rates of 20 frames per second or higher are supported). The picture is also large enough on a computer screen for details to be easily visible. Video captured at QVGA (320 x 240 pixels) or QQVGA (160 x 120 pixels) is really only suitable for emailing, although some people will find the playback size of QVGA video on a computer screen acceptable for certain purposes.

If you want to display your video clips on a TV set, look for a digicam that can capture video with sound at VGA resolution with a frame rate of 20 frames per second or higher. Cameras like this will provide you with video clips that can be edited and assembled using the same type of software as you would use for editing camcorder footage. In fact, in most cases, video from such a DSC can be inter-cut with camcorder footage and few people would notice any difference.

If you want video clips for emailing only, look for a DSC that offers QVGA or QQVGA capture as both will provide you with low-resolution files that are easy to send. You may need to increase the compression ratio to obtain files that are small enough to send but long enough to enjoy. A frame rate of 15 frames per second should not appear unnecessarily jerky, although it won't be as smooth as 20 frames per second.

Check the codec (AVI/Motion, JPEG or QuickTime) on your computer to be sure it can can handle video files in that format (most modern PCs should). Be prepared to invest in a high-capacity memory card (at least 256 MB) so you have enough storage capacity for video recordings.

Choosing a camcorder

With the price of some digital camcorders falling below A$1000 the video camera market is more strongly focused on digital capture than the still camera market and it has become quite difficult to find analogue camcorders. The reason for the shift to digital is simple: digital video (DV) offers better picture and audio quality, thanks to component colour sampling that captures three times as much colour information, Time Base Correction that eliminates jitters and automatic error correction that ensures seamless 'footage'. Copies (and copies of copies) of digital videos are as sharp as the original and digital video is easy to transfer to a computer for editing and sharing.

Camcorder buyers have four different types of camcorder to choose from:

MiniDV camcorders

These are by far the most popular and, generally, the most competitively priced. They record onto special MiniDV tape which is incompatible with home VCRs, so you have to dub the tapes from the camera onto a VHS tape when you want to share or archive recorded 'footage' by this means. Tapes are available in lengths that range from 30 to 180 minutes. An increasing number of MiniDV camcorders now support still image capture and many have memory card slots for this purpose. If the ability to make prints from still shots from these cameras is important, look for a model with at least 2-megapixel sensor resolution. Stills from such models can be printed to snapshot size. Resolutions of up to 3-megapixels are available from MiniDV camcorders but the number of camera settings is normally much less than a compact 3-megapixel DSC will offer.

Canon MV750i

Digital8 camcorders

These were a 'bridging' product that grew out of the top end of the analogue market and they continue to provide a transition from analogue to digital video capture. Unlike MiniDV camcorders, they record digital video onto Hi8 tapes (which are cheaper) and can also playback analogue recordings made on Hi8 and 8mm tapes. This makes them a good choice for buyers with a pre-existing collection of analogue Hi8 and 8mm tapes and those who can't afford a MiniDV camcorder. The main problem with this format is that few manufacturers support it, which means Digital8 camcorders can be hard to find. They also tend to be larger than MiniDV camcorders with similar specifications.

Sony DCR-TRV460

DVD camcorders

These were introduced by Hitachi several years ago, with Sony and Panasonic joining the market in 2003. The advantages of DVD capture include the ability to record stills and video on the same disk, easy playback of disks on home DVD players and extensive in-camera editing facilities that allow users to define the playback

Sony DVD201

order of recorded clips and have them play back seamlessly (without pauses while the playback head searches for the next clip). DVD camcorders can also capture still shots and store them on the same disk as video clips, however shot resolution is limited by the resolution of the camera's CCD sensor.

The MicroMV tape format

Sony, the inventor of this format, is the only company to release camcorders using it. The 60-minute tapes are 70% smaller than MiniDV tapes and recordings are compressed using MPEG-2 compression. The few cameras that are available are very small in size but highly sophisticated. Designed for PC connectivity and interoperability, they come with iLINK, Memory Stick and USB streaming and 1–2 megapixel sensors. Most models in Sony's range include communications facilities, allowing them to link to the Internet via a data-capable mobile phone. Like MiniDV recordings, clips taken with a MicroMV camcorder have to be dubbed to VHS tape for sharing.

Sony DCR-IP1

Note: digital video recordings can be viewed directly on most recent computer systems when the camcorder is connected by either USB 2.0 or FireWire cable (which is normally supplied with the camera), regardless of whether they have been recorded on tape, disk or memory card.

Displaying video clips

Although it is normal for camcorder users to play back their recordings on a standard TV set, this facility is not necessarily available to DSC users, nor is it necessarily the best way to view the clips. When clips that were captured at 160 x 120 pixel resolution are played on a TV screen, the picture quality will be poor and, on some screen types, the pixel structure will be very noticeable. Clips captured at 640 x 480 pixels may fill the screen but if their frame rate was 15 frames per second or less, all movement will look slightly jerky.

When you display video clips on a computer screen, the capture resolution will dictate the size at which they are displayed. A typical 640 x 480 pixel clip (VGA) will take up roughly two-thirds of the screen area, while a 320 x 240 pixel clip (QVGA) will occupy about a sixth of the frame. In contrast, a 160 x 120 pixel clip (QQVGA) is effectively 'thumbnail' size and may not be large enough to make an impact on the average viewer. Examples are shown below.

From left to right: VGA, QVGA and QQVGA video playback sizes compared.

If you want to send video clips by email further problems arise, regardless of how the clips were captured. A typical 12-second video clip captured at 320 x 240 pixel resolution with a frame rate of 15 frames per second uses up approximately 1 MB, which is more than the total email allowance provided by some ISPs.

Cutting the frame rate back to 10 or 12 frames per second will reduce your file size by about 20% but it will probably also make the playback look jerky. This can be unsettling to some viewers. Resizing it to a lower resolution may make it too small to view.

Editing programs like Apple's iMovie or Windows Movie Maker, both of which are supplied with the relevant manufacturers' latest operating systems, allow you to reduce the length of video clips. You can also change clip resolutions and frame rates via programs like ArcSoft VideoImpression and Pixela ImageMixer, which are supplied with some DSCs. A few cameras also support in-camera editing but this facility should be used with care as the 'discarded' sections of clips are usually deleted from the file that is saved in the camera's memory. Major changes to clips are best carried out on copies of the clip that have been saved on your PC's hard drive. That way, if you make an unsatisfactory edit, you can easily return to the original file and start again.

Sound capture

Although DSCs that can capture sound with video clips normally record sound monaurally rather than in stereo, many such cameras offer voice annotation as a handy add-on function. This enables photographers to record a short 'sound bite' and add it to a still picture, either as the picture is being taken or when it's being played back (most cameras support both options). The sound data is stored with the image file and can be accessed in any playback system with audio facilities. Audio files are usually small; a 30-second voice clip takes up roughly 120 KB of memory. In some DSCs, this function is a stand-alone option and such cameras can be used as voice recorders (image capture is switched off), allowing users to store 40 minutes or more of voice 'notes' on a 16 MB memory card.

Most MiniDV camcorders have two audio settings: two-channel 48Khz/16bit or four-channel 32KHz/12bit audio. The four-channel mode allows you to dub an extra audio track onto the tape afterwards and should be used for all video that will be edited.

Basic shooting tips

Regardless of whether you use a DSC or camcorder, shooting video involves a different approach from shooting stills. A still image aims to capture an instant in time, while the purpose of video is to record a sequence of events and, thereby, tell a story. We can't provide more than the most basic of information on movie making in the space available, so we will cover the topic with a list of 'do' and 'don't' tips. These tips apply to both camcorders and DSCs.

- Try to approach each project with the aim of making the viewer feel as if they are part of the scene.
- Aim to record a beginning, middle and end to help you tell a coherent story.
- Endeavor to include some scene-setting material that gives viewers a 'framework' for the story.
- Keep the camera as still as possible while you are recording and aim to capture brief sequences that can be edited together to tell a story.
- Try to start shots just before the action begins and finish them when it's over. You can trim clips when editing the sequence and the extra sound can provide a useful overlap. It's much better than discovering you've missed a vital second at the beginning or end of a shot.
- Match the shooting style to the response you want to draw from the viewer. Pan shots can be great for establishing an ambience, close-ups draw the viewer's attention to detail, and a sequence of short clips creates an impression of urgency and activity.
- Take account of ambient light levels and put the camera on a tripod when light levels are low.

- Video lights can be added to most camcorders when photographers need to be mobile when they are shooting. Many camcorders come with built-in lights and some models include flash facilities for still capture.
- If your DSC can't record sound, capture an audio track on a separate tape recorder and dub it in at the editing stage. You can also add a voice-over or background music at the same time. (Video editing software will normally be required to produce an edited video that includes dubbed audio.)

Non-linear editing (NLE)

Non-linear-editing (NLE) is the term used to describe the process of editing videos on a computer and many camcorders and DSCs are supplied with software for this purpose. You simply download the digital video clips to your hard drive and then cut and rearrange the scenes along a timeline on the computer screen. Many software packages provide separate timelines for audio and voice-overs and most support 'drag-and-drop' rearrangement facilities. The latest Window and Mac operating systems come with basic video and image editing facilities included. Windows Movie Maker is provided in Windows Me and XP, while Apple iMovie is part of Apple's iLife suite and Apple bundles the more sophisticated Final Cut Express 2.0 software with some Macintosh PCs.

Some third-party editing packages that may be bundled with digital camcorders, DSCs or computer hardware such as CD/DVD burners and FireWire cards include 'Light' editions of Pinnacle Studio (RRP A$249), and Ulead Video Studio (RRP A$180). Adobe Premiere Elements (RRP A$179) was released in late 2004 and may be bundled with some future cameras. All Canon camcorders are supplied with the Australian-developed Video-Presenter movie creation software. Pixela ImageMixer is another bundled application that includes both video and still image editing and works with MPEG movie clips. ArcSoft VideoImpression (sold separately for US$49.99), Roxio EasyMedia Creator (RRP US$79.95) and VideoWave (RRP US $49.95) are other popular bundled applications.

Details of the above applications and, in some cases, trial downloads, can be obtained from the following websites:

ArcSoft VideoImpression:
http://www.arcsoft.com/en/products/videoimpression.

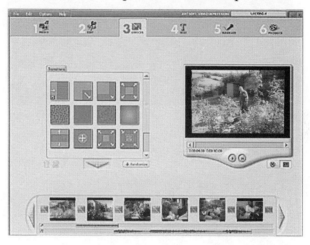

Canon VideoPresenter: http://www.canon.com.au

Pinnacle Studio: http://www.pinnaclesys.com.

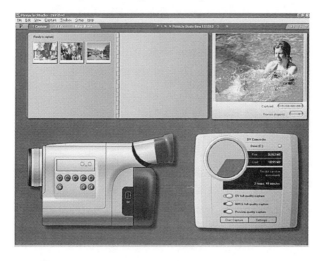

Roxio VideoWave: www.roxio.com.

Ulead VideoStudio: http://www.ulead.com.

Most consumers will be happier with cheaper NLE software that is extremely easy to use and great for beginners, but has limited power and functionality.

Interesting Fact #8

With many households adding a DVD player to their home entertainment equipment, digital photographers have a new, easy and enjoyable way to share their pictures with other family members and friends. Most recently released DVD players can play JPEG images that have been stored on CD or DVD disks. This allows you to create slideshows from your digital pictures and display them on your TV set. Note: no DVD player that we are aware of can display other file types so, if your pictures are in RAW or TIFF format they must be converted to JPEG before you download them to a disk.

Instructions for creating slideshows, screensavers and 'wall-paper' for your computer can be found in Chapter 12.

You can also create your own Video CDs (VCD) and DVDs. The process involves two basic steps:

1. Capturing and editing the movie, using a suitable software application (see above).
2. Converting this movie into VCD compliant MPEG format.

Some of the software applications listed above can handle this conversion, though not necessarily with all PC operating systems. Look for programs that include 'MPEG rendering' to find which ones provide this facility. Special DVD-burning applications like Adaptec's RecordNow! Deluxe (RRP US$49.99) and MyDVD Studio Video Edition, which includes some editing facilities (RRP US$69.99) are ideal.

Note: prices are approximate and were correct at the time of printing.

Chapter 9

Image defects

The quality of pictures produced by digital still and video cameras has improved dramatically with the increase in sensor resolution and development of better image data processing algorithms. However, digital photographers still need to be aware of certain system-related problems that can cause their digital pictures to look less than perfect. Some are easily prevented, while others are inherent in the equipment and may not be avoidable, although most can be minimised.

Inadequate resolution is the most frequent reason for poor image quality. The problem arises mainly among newcomers to digital photography because photographers attempt to fit as many images as possible onto the memory card supplied with the camera. The resulting pictures may look satisfactory on screen, but when a 60 KB image captured at VGA resolution is printed out, the resulting quality will be very poor, even at snapshot size. Enlarging the image to the point where individual pixels begin to appear creates 'jaggies' (noticeable stair-steps) along diagonal lines and edges in the picture.

Jaggies

Fortunately, jaggies are easy for digital photographers to avoid: simply shoot with the camera's highest resolution and quality settings and don't enlarge the image beyond the 'acceptable' dimensions for the sensor's resolution (see page 20 for details). On the occasions low-resolution capture is needed, the image processors in most recent DSCs include anti-aliasing algorithms that smooth out obvious jagged edges. Similar algorithms are provided in some editing software. Both will have a 'softening' effect on the image. Do not attempt to counteract this softening by sharpening the image with the in-camera sharpness adjustment or in editing software. Sharpening makes jaggies more obvious, so it should be avoided when pictures are captured at low resolution for emailing.

Jaggies are a resolution-related imaging problem that can be easily avoided by shooting with the highest resolution and quality settings.

Compression artefacts

When compression is used to make image files smaller, images often end up looking quite blocky. This is due to the way the most common compression system, JPEG, works (described under Interesting Fact #9 on page 126). The more the information is compressed, the more obvious these blocks become until individual blocks are clearly outlined, creating 'compression artefacts'.

One useful feature of JPEG compression is that it allows photographers to control the degree of compression applied. This

Compression artefacts

is done via the 'quality' setting in most DSCs and better editing software. Whereas cameras tend to have only two or three JPEG compression levels, it is common for software to provide 10–12 JPEG settings, ranging from minimal compression (which discards between one-third and half of the data) to very high compression levels (which can reduce the file size by 70–90%). At the highest 'quality' settings on a top quality DSC, it can be difficult to tell the JPEG copy from an uncompressed original. Compression strategies in editing software can vary; some software applications show the compression as percentages, while others use a sliding scale from 0 to 12. The differences between high and low compression settings also vary. It is not uncommon to find JPEG files reduced to one-twentieth of the original file size or less. By the time the lowest JPEG setting is reached, the compression ratio is so high that JPEG blocks are visible with minimal enlargement.

JPEG compression produces different file sizes with different types of photographs. Photographs of detailed subjects cannot be compressed as much as those with large, areas of unstructured colour (such as an expanse of sky). For example, a high-resolution JPEG file from a 6-megapixel DSC can be less than 2 MB in size for a subject with minimal detail, whereas a shot with intricate detail can be over 5 MB in size. Care must be taken to match the degree of compression to the subject matter to ensure detailed subjects are captured without compression artefacts. The highest quality settings should be used wherever possible, particularly with detailed subjects.

While more sophisticated DSCs may offer uncompressed RAW and TIFF image capture in addition to JPEG, the majority of point-and-shoot models only capture JPEG files. This can create some problems for camera users who wish to edit their pictures because JPEG compression is a one-way street. Each time you open and resave a JPEG image file, some data will be lost. Eventually, the effect of the repeated data compression will be visible and the image will be unusable. Note: when saving images that you plan to edit, always edit and resave your digital photograph in the editing software's native file format (*.psd for Adobe, *.pct for Apple, *ufo for Ulead, *.png for Microsoft) or use an uncompressed, universally recognised file format, such as TIFF or bitmap.

Sharpening artefacts

Sharpening artefacts show up as black or white halos around contrasting areas of the image. They can be produced by applying sharpening at any stage of the imaging process, from capture to output. Where possible, sharpening artefacts should be avoided as they can spoil an otherwise excellent digital photograph. Unfortunately, some cheaper DSCs automatically introduce quite strong sharpening as a standard part of their image-processing algorithms. This can be overcome to some degree by moving the sharpness control to the lowest setting (if the camera permits). Better quality cameras tend to have more normal sharpness levels and artefacts are only produced when the sharpness is set to the highest level or when additional sharpening is applied in editing software.

Note: you cannot undo the effects of in-camera sharpening in editing software as the only tool available to reduce image

The pictures above provide a comparison between an image without sharpening artefacts (left) and one that has been over-sharpened (right). Note the black and white haloes along the edges in the over-sharpened picture.

sharpness is the Blur tool, which simply softens the image. For this reason, it is best to delay sharpening until you are editing the image because most software allows you to go back and cancel the effect if it's not what you want.

Image noise

Noise in a digital photograph commonly appears as granularity or a pattern of tiny white or coloured dots scattered randomly across the image. It's a reasonably good indication of the quality of the sensor and the camera's data processing algorithms. Noise is produced under a number of circumstances: when the number of photons (the fundamental 'particles' of light) striking the sensor is very low, when the temperature of the sensor is high, through errors in the transmission of the signal from the sensor to the processor, and as part of the signal amplification process. It can be difficult to determine precisely what caused the noise in a particular image but it is safe to assume that several of the above factors were responsible.

While all digital camera sensors are subject to noise problems, some cameras are more noise-prone than others and the majority of compact cameras will show some noise in long time exposures at high ISO settings (ISO 400 and above). Although effective image

The pictures above show an image without obvious noise (left) and one that is noise-affected (right). Note the speckling in the picture on the right.

processing can reduce noise levels to some degree, cameras with small sensors and high photosite densities are very noise-prone. Sensor size, coupled with effective resolution, can provide a guide to a camera's noise susceptibility when it is used in relatively low light levels. DSLRs with larger photosites can capture more incoming photons and are less likely to be affected by noise than compact digicams. The tables in Appendix 2 provide a guide to the sensor dimensions for most common sensor sizes, along with typical photosite sizes for different resolution levels.

Pixel errors

Given the small size of DSC image sensors, it is not surprising that occasional manufacturing errors occur and sensors are released onto the market with photodiodes that don't perform correctly. As long as there aren't too many of them, most cameras' image processors can interpolate around the defective photosites and produce a digital image that, for all practical purposes, contains all the information required to create a perfect image. However, when light levels are low and the electronic gain is increased to boost the strength of the signals from the photosites, defective photodiodes can show up as 'pixel errors' that appear as white, black or coloured dots, slightly larger than the normal pixel size. Unlike regular image noise, pixel errors produce the same dot pattern in every shot in which they are visible.

Pixel errors cause pixels to become stuck as this picture illustrates. Note the granularity in the picture due to high image noise levels.

Noise reduction systems

Most DSC manufacturers use some form of image processing to minimise both pixel errors and noise problems. In some cases it's done as part of the image processing and the only thing the photographer notices is the additional time it takes to process and store shots. In other cases, a process known as 'dark frame subtraction' is used. This causes the camera to take two sequential shots, the first with the sensor covered and the second to expose the picture. The 'dark' frame records the inherent noise pattern of the sensor and this is subtracted mathematically from the image data in the recorded shot.

Any camera movement that occurs between the two shots will lead to a blurring of the subject and the noise reduction will fail. Consequently the camera must be mounted on a tripod whenever this type of noise reduction is used. Dark frame subtraction is seldom perfect, but it often eliminates stuck pixels and may produce a substantial reduction in image noise.

Other manufacturers use smoothing algorithms to identify and eliminate noise patterns in captured image data. This can double data processing times and increase the delay between when you press the shutter release and when the image is stored in memory. Note: JPEG compression makes images that were originally noisy look much worse so if your camera offers RAW or TIFF capture it should be used for all long time exposures.

Coloured fringing

Although poor-quality lenses can cause coloured fringes to appear in digital photographs, a more common cause is the overflow of data between photosites (an effect known as '*blooming*'). This often occurs when a digital camera is pointed towards a source of bright light. It is particularly obvious in shots that show dark branches or leaves backlit against a bright sky (and shots of this type are an excellent guide to both the optical quality and the sensor performance in a digital camera). Blooming is reasonably common in cheaper compact DSCs but rare in DSLR cameras and its effects are difficult (or even impossible) to eliminate.

Many sensor manufacturers have introduced anti-blooming gates, which drain excess charge from each row of pixels (in much the same way as ditches can drain excess water from flooded fields). These anti-blooming gates work well under most conditions but can seldom handle really strong backlighting (which is one reason for not pointing a camera towards the sun when taking pictures unless there is an intervening object that prevents light from shining directly into the lens).

Another source of coloured fringing is chromatic aberration, which is associated with the camera's lens and occurs when the lens fails to focus light of different wavelengths at the same point on the image plane. The development of new types of low-dispersion glass has allowed lens manufacturers to minimise chromatic aberration. Achromatic and apochromatic lenses use compensating elements to bring the different wavelengths of light together so they image on the same plane. In the case of achromatic lenses, blue and red wavelengths are involved. Apochromatic lenses add green correction and superachromatic lenses correct for four or more wavelength bands, effectively eliminating colour errors. Naturally, costs increase as the optics become more sophisticated.

Flare

Flare is caused by light reflections within the lens. This problem is most commonly seen in photographs where the lens has been pointed towards a bright light source. The reflections can be produced from any surface where glass meets air (such as the front or rear surface of the lens) and it's often the lights just outside the image area, which you don't necessarily notice when composing your shot, that cause the biggest problems. The problem appears as an overall haze that obscures subject detail or as pale yellowish-

Flare is most common in shots taken with the lens pointing towards a source of light.

orange streaks or geometric spots (reflecting the shape of the camera's iris diaphragm) that are dispersed across the frame. In top-quality lenses, flare is minimal and, although modern lens coatings and well-designed lens hoods can reduce flare to very low levels, nothing can totally eliminate it.

Preventing flare is relatively easy if you can use a properly designed lens hood for all outdoor shooting. Many compact DSCs lack this facility, although most models with longer zoom lenses are supplied with lens hoods. Flare can be a serious problem for photographers whose cameras have electronic viewfinders because the viewing area can be interrupted by wide streaks of brilliant white or pale yellow. This can make EVFs difficult to use for backlit photography, though the streaks seldom appear in the actual shots. LCD screens can also be flare affected and will usually be difficult to view in such conditions.

To avoid flare, don't point your camera into the sun or, if you really want to take backlit shots, be prepared to experiment and delete the shots that didn't work when you're able to evaluate them properly.

A special type of flare can be produced by foreign matter on the surface of the camera's lens. When the camera is pointed towards

Flare spots caused by dried droplets of salt water on the lens.

a bright light source, particles of dust or salt or greasy streaks will disperse the light, creating bright spots and streaks across the picture. Keeping lenses clean will minimise this problem.

Moiré

Moiré is a pattern produced by interference between repeating patterns in a subject, such as closely spaced parallel lines and some finely patterned fabrics, and the receptors on the sensor used to capture the image. It is particularly common when patterns with very closely spaced elements are sampled at low resolution. Moiré patterns are most commonly seen when digital photographs are viewed on a computer screen or TV set at low resolution. They are seldom visible when images are printed, particularly if the resolution level is high.

You can sometimes detect moiré when you enlarge a section of the image on the camera's monitor in playback mode, but this cannot be considered a reliable guide to whether the shot contains moiré, as changing the viewing magnification will usually cause it to disappear. The best ways to avoid moiré are to:

1. Shoot at the highest capture resolution and quality.
2. Use a small lens aperture.
3. Vary the distance between the subject and the camera lens and the camera angle until the effect disappears.
4. Use a slower shutter speed.

Moiré can also appear when images are scanned, so it pays to scan at a higher resolution than you require, then resample the image using an interpolation-based method that takes account of groups of pixels (such as bicubic resampling). This is more effective than a simple pixel resize method that merely selects a subset of the original pixels to create a smaller image. Most better quality editing applications support resampling when downsizing.

Distortion

Very few compact digicam lenses can produce images that are totally distortion-free, although the degree to which they are affected by distortion is unlikely to be of concern to the majority of photographers. In most cameras, the effect of distortion is only visible in close-up shots taken with the lens at its widest zoom setting. Even then, the degree of distortion is usually small.

Distortion comes in two forms: pincushioning, which causes horizontal and vertical lines to bend inwards, and barrel distortion, which has the opposite effect. The latter is more common and changing the lens aperture has no effect on the degree of distortion. It is only significant when you need to photograph small subjects where precise reproduction of subject dimensions is required. In such cases, special macro or copying lenses should be used (even if you have to capture on film and scan the end result to obtain a digital picture).

Interesting Fact #9

JPEG works by separating the image data into two subsets: colour and detail. Colour data is compressed more than detail because the human eye can detect small deviations in detail more readily than colour changes. The compression process also sorts image detail into fine and coarse detail and discards the finest details first because our eyes are more attuned to coarse detail. JPEG can allow image files to be reduced by a factor of 10 or more with little apparent loss in picture quality (depending on how much the resulting images are enlarged for viewing). The compression algorithms work on blocks of 8 x 8 pixels, which are compressed independently. As more compression is applied, individual blocks of pixels become visible, defined by fine hair-like lines surrounding each block. These are known as JPEG artefacts. If individual pixels are visible when you enlarge an image on a computer screen, the image has been over-compressed. More information is discarded as compression ratios rise and there comes a point where the effects of the compression are visible with even moderate enlargement. By this time, pictures are totally unprintable, and probably unusable for viewing larger than thumbnail size.

Chapter 10

Digitising without a camera

You don't need a digital camera to obtain pictures in digital format; photographs captured on film are easily converted into digital form by scanning. Many photolabs offer a scan-to-CD service for films they process and, in the main, this is a cost-effective option for people who only need to digitise shots occasionally. Most labs charge between A$8 and A$15 per film if the scanning is done when the films are processed. Actual prices will vary depending on the number of films in the batch and the speed of the service. Many labs will charge less to scan several films at a time to one CD and many charge a premium for a while-you-wait or one-hour service.

Why stick with film?

Although the latest digital cameras can match (and often exceed) the performance of film cameras, there are still some times when better results can be obtained by shooting on film. The main reasons to use a film camera are:

1. To obtain a wider angle of view. This mainly applies to SLR camera users as the angles of view provided by most current compact DSCs are comparable to similarly featured compact

film cameras. However, only professional DSLR cameras can match the wide-angle capabilities of film SLRs because their sensors are the same size as a 35mm film frame. DSLR cameras priced below about A$3000 have between 30% and 40% less field of view when fitted with a standard 35mm lens.

2. When an instantaneous shutter response is required. Typical shutter lag times for digital cameras have improved dramatically in the past 12 months, and many cameras have delays as short as 0.2 seconds between when the photographer presses the shutter button and when the picture is taken. However, there are still some cameras with delays as long as one second. In contrast, all film cameras capture the shot when the shutter button is pressed unless the focusing system takes time to lock onto the subject (which also delays capture with digital cameras). Fast response times are advantageous when shooting sports or active children and they can help to minimise camera shake in low light conditions.

3. When high-volume continuous shooting is required. If you're taking a burst of shots on a film camera, the speed at which shots are taken and the number of shots in a burst are controlled by the film transport system and the length of the film in the camera. With a DSC, the size of the camera's buffer memory and the speed of its microprocessor control the number of frames that can be captured in a burst and the speed at which they can be captured. It is rare for digital cameras to match the frame rates of film cameras.

4. When you want to use selective focusing to isolate a subject from a potentially distracting background. DSCs have greater inherent depth-of-field than 35mm cameras with the same lens focal length. The problem is directly related to the size of the camera's sensor with respect to a 35mm film frame. When cameras with the smallest sensors (4 mm x 3 mm in area) are used, the depth-of-field is 9x that of a 35mm camera and everything in the shot will look sharp making selective focusing

impossible. In contrast, most digital SLR cameras have 1.5x or 1.6x the depth-of-field of a 35mm SLR and selective focusing can be achieved, particularly with telephoto lenses.

Why scan?

The main reason for scanning photographs is to convert them into a digitised form that can be used in computer applications. However, an increasing number of photographers are scanning prints and images captured on film to preserve them against the almost inevitable deterioration that occurs over time, especially to colour photos. Once photographs have been converted into digital form they are immune to the chemical changes that can produce fading and colour shifts in colour photographs and discolour black-and-white prints. Most computers come with CD burners and DVD burners are now available at prices that are affordable to many consumers, offering much higher storage capacities.

Digitised image files are relatively easy to 'migrate' to the latest storage technologies as they become available and they take up less space when stored on an optical disk. Digital photographs are also easier to print, either at home or at a photolab, because you can print straight from the file, without having to find and prepare a negative or slide. They can be easily included in documents like family histories, genealogical charts, cards, calendars and other printed items. It is also easy and cheap to provide copies of family photos on CD to other family members. This is becoming increasingly popular as more families acquire DVD players. Most recently released DVD players can playback JPEG images as a slideshow, making them accessible to a wider range of family members.

Scanners for home use

The main disadvantage of having your films scanned for you is that you have little or no control over the size of the resulting image files. A typical lab-scanned CD will hold roughly 100 JPEG image files, which means individual images will be around 700 KB in size. While these files should make good snapshot prints, they may not have high enough resolution to make good A4 enlargements. An alternative is to purchase a scanner and digitise your own pictures.

There are two main types of scanners: *flatbed scanners* that are designed to work with prints, artwork or documents and other non-transparent media and *film scanners* that convert film negatives or slides into digital files. Of the two, flatbed scanners are substantially cheaper and usually much more versatile, while film scanners generally offer the highest resolution. Some recently released flatbed scanners come with, or will accept, a film scanning adaptor that allows you to scan slides and negatives. The quality of these scanners has improved dramatically in the past year and the best can match the performance of dedicated film scanners.

Most flatbed scanners can also be used for scanning printed text and many are supplied with Optical Character Recognition (OCR) software, which converts the scanned data into a text file that can be edited with any word processing program. The results may not be completely accurate, but the small number of errors produced

A flatbed scanner that can scan both prints and films can be purchased for less than A$350. Note the film holders on the right.

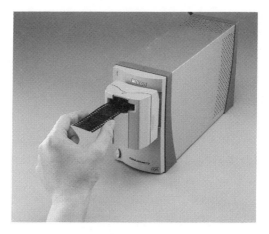

Dedicated film scanners can accept both mounted slides and film strips. Prices for these scanners start at around A$1000 but they usually deliver higher resolution and better colour accuracy than flatbed scanners.

by most OCR programs when they encounter unfamiliar type styles or words will usually be easy to correct.

Scanner buying guide

If you plan to buy a scanner, consider the following:

1. Whether you are more likely to scan prints or flat artworks (paintings and drawings) than films (negatives and slides). This will help you to decide whether to buy a flatbed or film scanner.
2. How much you are prepared to spend. Although high output quality comes at a price, it should be possible to buy a flatbed scanner that will meet most amateur photographers' needs for less than A$400 and a model to suit enthusiasts for under A$800.
3. The compatibility requirements of your personal computer. Scanners cannot be used as stand-alone devices but most are compatible with Windows and Mac operating systems and many will also work with Unix and Linux.

4. The scanner's output resolution (see the *Understanding Scanner Specifications* box in this chapter).

5. Check the user interface, looking for useful features such as the ability to scan individual prints from a selection on the platen and the ability to straighten skewed prints automatically when scanning. Many scanners also include useful cropping controls, descreening filters (for scanning printed pages) and one-touch scanning to software applications or an email facility. These can be valuable time-savers for busy photographers.

6. Look carefully at the bundled software. Most scanners are supplied with drivers for Windows and Mac PCs plus basic image editing applications. Some have built-in dust removal software and colour restoration, while others provide support for scanning directly to a printer. Other business-related applications, such as OCR and PDF (Portable Document Format) conversion software, may also be provided for scanning printed text.

7. If you plan to scan old colour prints, find out whether the scanner software includes a colour restoration application (many do) or provides adjustments for colour balance, contrast and brightness. These will normally be required to bring faded prints back to acceptable colour levels. Note: some of these problems can be corrected with image editing software, but you generally get the best end results if you start with a 'clean', colour-accurate scan.

8. If you plan to scan old black-and-white photos, check that the scanner can handle stippled paper (which was very popular in the 1960s to 1970s). Many scanners produce blotchy results with this style of paper. Enlarging a small section of a scanned print to 200% will show if the scanner is up to the task.

9. Make sure the scanner is supplied with everything you need to connect it to your computer and start scanning. Some scanners are not supplied with USB cables. Although these are rela- tively cheap (under A$10) it is annoying to unpack the scanner

Canon Australia

Flatbed scanners that can be mounted vertically will save desktop space.

and find you have to return to the shops to buy a cable before you can use it.

10. Make sure the scanner will fit on your desk so it's ready to use when you need it. Some flatbed scanners come with cradles that allow them to be used vertically. These can be significant space-savers when desktop real estate is limited.

11. Finally, select a scanner with the highest *optical* (not '*optimised*') resolution you can afford. Scanning resolution is normally expressed in dots per inch (dpi) so the higher this figure, the higher the resolution you can achieve in your scans. This is particularly important if you plan to use a flatbed scanner for film scanning, where the small size of the original means a considerable degree of enlargement is required to make an A4-sized print. You can find more information about buying a scanner on the *CHOICE* website (www.choice.com.au).

Understanding Scanner Specifications

Most scanners work by either passing a linear image sensor across the image to be scanned or moving the image under the scanning sensor. Hence, the number of image recording elements (photo-receptors or 'pixels') in the sensor head determines the optical horizontal resolution of the device. The most common horizontal resolution for flatbed scanners is 1200 dots/inch (dpi), which means there should be 1200 photo-receptors in the scanner's head. The optical vertical resolution is determined by the number of steps the scanner head takes to scan the entire platen, or scanning area. The most common vertical resolution for flatbed scanners is 1400 dpi.

Many scanners claim higher resolutions than the quoted optical resolution and it is easy for non-specialist consumers to be confused by the figures quoted in advertising materials. Be cautious about manufacturers' literature that gives the scanner's performance in 'optimised' resolution figures. 'Optimised' usually means interpolated and the output quality may not be quite as high as the claims suggest. Interpolated scans are the same as interpolated photographs: the larger files are created by adding extra pixels based on the characteristics of existing pixels in the image. They do not add any detail that was not captured in the original scan.

A scanner's optical resolution is the best guide to the amount of detail it can capture and provides the best guide to output quality. However, done well, interpolation can be useful. It can allow small, detailed pictures to be enlarged without significant quality loss, provided the end result is printed with the correct parameters for viewing it. For scanning 35mm films, an optical horizontal resolution of 3200 dpi or higher is recommended if the images are to be printed to A4 size or larger. For snapshot-sized prints, an optical resolution of 1200 dpi is ideal for producing same-sized prints, while 2400 dpi is required for an A4-sized enlargement.

Scanner buyers also need to be aware of the importance of

bit depth, which determines the number of colour gradations a scanner can record. The more gradations you can capture, the more subtle the tonal range in the scanned image can be and the better the chance of obtaining accurate colour reproduction. For colour scanning, at least 24-bit capability is required to match the number of colours the human eye can resolve. Twenty-four-bit scanners produce images by combining 256 levels of each of the three primary colours: red, green and blue. The result is an image with 16.7 million colour gradations, which is all the eye can discern. If your scanner allows you to select the bit depth for your scans, it's best to select 8 bits per colour channel (or 24-bit) for all colour work because all software applications can handle this bit depth. Note: the bit depth figures quoted in advertising materials generally refer to the total colour bit depth (i.e. 8 bits each for red, green and blue) not the bit depth for individual colour channels.

Many flatbed scanners on the market boast higher bit depths, with 48-bit (or 3x 12-bit) being the most common. However, this is not necessarily an advantage to digital snap-shooters. There's little point in paying a premium price for a high-end scanner if you're not prepared to invest in an editing application that can use it (only Adobe Photoshop and Photoshop Elements 3.0 and Ulead PhotoImpact 8 supported higher bit depths when this book was published). Note: when scanning black-and-white photo graphs, an 8-bit scanner is all that is required to capture the entire tonal gamut because you have only one colour channel (black to white) to deal with.

Preparing photos for scanning

The most common cause of poor quality scans is dust, lint or hairs on the surface of either the original photograph or the scanning platen or scan head. Such contamination is picked up by the scanner and included in the image file and it can take hours of painstaking retouching to remove it. Although many recently released scanners come with dust and scratch removal software, its use adds substantially to the amount of time each scan takes. Try to avoid problems by working with clean originals and a dust-free scanner.

Use an anti-static blower brush or compressed air spray (available from most photo shops) to remove loose particles from prints or films before they are scanned. Dust on the platen is best removed by cleaning it with an antistatic cloth but any cleaning must be carried out with care to avoid scratching the surface of the platen. Try to work in a clean, dust-free environment and handle your originals in a way that will ensure they are not recontaminated.

If your scanner is supplied with software that will eliminate dust and scratch marks automatically, use it for films that you have been unable to clean with the air brush. If this isn't effective, you can eradicate larger dust particles and hairs from scanned photos with the clone tool in your editing software, as long as there aren't too many of them. However, the process is time-consuming and the results are seldom as good as you obtain by working with clean originals.

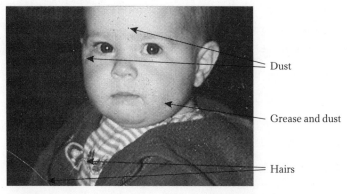

Dust

Grease and dust

Hairs

Dust, hairs and grease on the platen of the scanner can affect image files. When there are too many defects to remove easily, the scan becomes unusable.

Preparing the scanner

All scanners are supplied with basic driver software. Sometimes this software can be accessed independently but it's generally best to call up the image in an editing program using the File>Import control. If you have loaded the software supplied with the scanner, it will appear in the drop-down menu. Selecting it will usually cause a preview of the image to be scanned to appear on your computer screen. However, sometimes you have to initiate this pre-scan. Use it to check that the scanning parameters have been set properly and that the image is correctly aligned and properly orientated (it's surprisingly easy to put films on the platen upside-down!). Some drivers will automatically reorientate skewed prints and set the scanning area to the optimal print dimensions before they scan. Others require you to do this manually. Most also allow you to flip pictures horizontally or vertically and crop the image, if required.

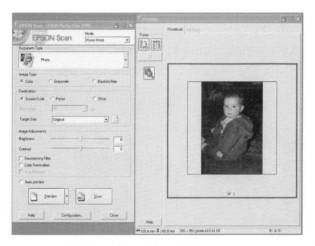

A typical scanner graphical user interface (GUI) showing a preview screen.

Matching resolution to output

When scanning images for printing, the best results will be obtained when you match the scan resolution to the print output.

Calculating the correct scanning resolution is relatively easy, as long as all dimensions use the same system of measurement. You simply divide the shorter dimension of the desired output size by the same dimension on the picture you are scanning and multiply that figure by the recommended output resolution.

For example, if you have a 100 mm x 125 mm print that you want to enlarge and print out on your inkjet printer at A4 size (210 x 297 mm), the calculation is as follows:

$21 \div 10 = 2.1$

If you want to print at the recommended resolution of 300 dpi, you will need to start with at least 600 dpi resolution in order to enlarge the image to A4 size. Note: because the aspect ratio (relationship of the horizontal and vertical dimensions) of a sheet of A4 paper is different from the aspect ratio of a 100 mm x 125 mm print, some cropping will be required. For this reason, we have based our calculations on the shorter side as it ensures the picture will fit entirely (it is easy to trim off excess paper). If your original is a 35mm negative or slide, you will need a resolution of 2700 dpi to achieve the same output quality at A4 size. Note: many scanner drivers give you the option of setting the input size plus the desired dimensions. They will then calculate and apply the correct resolution settings for the scan.

Scanning at a higher resolution than you plan to use is not usually recommended because large files use up significant amounts of disk space in your computer and take a long time to scan. However, if you plan to edit your pictures in one of the popular software applications, starting with an uncompressed high-resolution image can be advantageous as the file contains all the pictorial and colour data the scanner captured. Most editing software will allow you to save scanned images in an uncompressed (or losslessly compressed) native file format that allows them to be opened and worked on repeatedly without sacrificing image data. Examples include *.psd for Photoshop,. *.psp for Jasc Paint Shop Pro, *.png for Microsoft and *.ufo for Ulead.

Avoid saving your images in JPEG format while you're still working on them because JPEG is a lossy compression format. This means you lose picture information *each time* you edit and resave the file (although not if you simply open the file for viewing and make no changes to it). The higher the compression level— and the more times the file is edited and resaved—the greater the loss of image quality. To preserve the highest picture quality when editing images in a software application, save your files in TIFF format or the program's default uncompressed file format rather than as JPEGs.

Always keep an uncompressed, high resolution copy of each original image file (duplicated on CD-ROM, if possible) to preserve optimum image quality for the next time you want to use the picture. You can always reduce the file size after you've worked on it.

Interesting Fact #10

TWAIN is a standard application protocol that allows image processing software to interact with devices like digital cameras and scanners. Special 'TWAIN driver' software is required for each device but all must meet the agreed standard laid down by the TWAIN Working Group. The licence is available free of charge to manufacturers and details can be found at www.twain.org.

The first TWAIN standard was established in 1992 and the latest iteration of the standard was version 1.9, which was released in January 2000. The word TWAIN was derived from Rudyard Kipling's poem, *The Ballad of East and West*, which contains the famous line: "...and never the twain shall meet...". It reflected the difficulty of connecting scanners and personal computers in the late 1980s and early 1990s. Shortly after being adopted, it was capitalised to make it more distinctive. This led people to believe it was an acronym, and then to a contest to come up with an explanatory expansion. None was selected, but the entry 'Technology Without An Interesting Name' continues to haunt the standard.

Chapter 11

Printing and managing images

As little as 50 years ago, most photographers worked in black-and-white, and did their own processing and printing. This led many of them to become expert darkroom operators and created a considerable amount of respect for the craft of photographic printing. However, the difficulties and expense associated with producing black-and-white prints put amateur photographers off and home-based darkrooms were relatively rare. With the advent of colour film, home printing became even more challenging as the materials were more expensive and they degraded quite quickly. Some dangerous chemicals were also involved.

While the proliferation of colour film and cost-competitiveness of lab-based processing opened photography to a much wider user group, the complexity of colour processing and printing made even professional photographers lab-dependent and took many aspects of image presentation away from the primary picture-taker. The shift to digital cameras has returned control to the hands of photographers because some of the latest printers make it possible for just about anybody to make good colour prints at home. While consumers are increasingly bombarded by advertising telling how easy it is 'to make great prints from your digital photos' using the latest home printer, simply buying a printer and connecting it to your PC and/or camera does not guarantee you will obtain good-looking prints.

Furthermore, although being able to produce photo prints at home is an attractive concept, it is not necessarily the best or most cost-effective way to print digital pictures. Currently, numerous photo processors are competing for business, both in local shopping centres and online, and there are some attractive-sounding options available. It has become quite difficult for non-specialists to choose between these options in terms of both the cost of making prints and the quality of the end result, so we will begin by carrying out a cost benefit analysis on the most commonly available ways of printing digital photography.

Printing at a photolab

Having digital snapshots printed by your local photolab is currently the cheapest and most convenient option for most consumers. You simply call into the lab with one of the following:

1. your digital camera with the image files in memory
2. the memory card from your digital camera
3. a CD or Zip disk onto which you have downloaded the shots you wish to print
4. a USB drive onto which you have downloaded the shots you wish to print.

Many Australian photolabs have installed self-service kiosks where consumers can plug in a memory card or the device that contains the images. They can then use the display screen to select which shots they want to print. In many cases, voice prompts are provided by the kiosk, while in some locations, staff at the store will help new users to place their orders. Customers can choose whether to print selected photos at standard snapshot size, order enlarge-ments or have selected images burned to CD. In some locations, selected shots can be emailed direct from the kiosk to friends and

Many photolabs have self-serve kiosks where digital photographers can download image files and have them printed and/or archived to an optical disk.

family members or posted in password-protected albums on the Internet. Some kiosks also allow customers to crop pictures, correct red eyes in flash photos or add fancy borders or text messages.

The orders placed via the kiosk are sent directly to the processing equipment and many labs can fulfil small orders (up to 20 prints) in 15–20 minutes. In most cases, the prints are made on traditional photographic paper and the results should be as good as prints from cameras that use film. Print costs are normally the same as the cost of reprints from 35mm negatives, although some labs charge a little less (because they don't have to process film before printing) and many offer discounted prices for large orders. For snapshot-sized prints, this option is usually the cheapest overall.

Printing at home

For home printing, digital photographers can choose between two quite different technologies: inkjet and thermal dye transfer. Inkjet

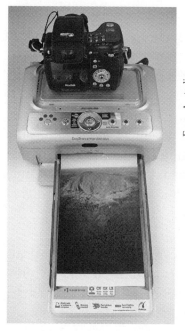

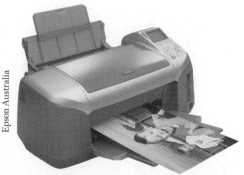

Home printer choices: (left) thermal printers that produce snapshot-sized prints and (right) inkjet printers that produce A4 prints but can also print on snapshot-sized paper. Both types include models that can print directly from connected digital cameras.

printers are very popular because they are cheap to purchase, and easy to connect to a computer and use. Ink cartridges and papers are widely available and, in the main, competitively priced. Thermal dye transfer technology (also known as 'dye sublimation') replaces the ink cartridges in an inkjet printer with a cartridge containing dye-impregnated ribbons. Heat is used to transfer the dyes to the specially treated paper in three passes. The yellow dye is laid down first, then the magenta and finally cyan, after which the print is covered with a layer of encapsulating plastic that protects the dyes against environmental contaminants.

Whereas the majority of inkjet printers have been designed for printing on A4-sized paper, most under-A$400 thermal printers are designed for snapshot-sized (or smaller) prints. Thermal printers that can produce A4-sized prints are available but, with prices in the thousands of dollars, they are not designed for consumer applications and inkjets remain the best choice for photographers who want A4-sized or larger prints (A3 inkjet printers are available with prices ranging from around A$600 to over A$1000).

The options for printing digital photos at home changed rapidly at the end of 2003 when the first PictBridge printers arrived. Pict-Bridge is a new standard that was developed to provide an easy way for consumers to connect a digital camera to a printer and make prints without requiring a computer. This was not the first time direct printing had been developed, but it was the first time direct printing was possible between a wide variety of digital cameras and printers, regardless of which manufacturer the devices came from.

Camera users simply connect their camera to the printer using the supplied USB cable, switch both devices on and use the camera's LCD screen and menu system to select images for printing and input the number of prints from each shot. In some cases you can choose from a range of page formats (2, 4, 6 or more prints per page); in others images may be cropped and resized. Some systems allow users to print a date stamp on selected shots. Canon was the first company to market DSCs and printers with PictBridge capability but by early 2004 the overwhelming majority of new DSCs and printers released for sale were PictBridge enabled and it is becoming difficult to find products without Pict-Bridge capability.

Although PictBridge has done a lot to make home printing easier and more accessible to ordinary consumers, there are a few downsides to direct printing from a digital camera:

1. The only way of viewing the image you want to print is on the camera's monitor. Most camera LCD screens are very small and very few of them will show you the exact image colours, contrast levels or saturation as they will appear in the final print. It can also be difficult to determine whether the shot is in focus (though you can use the playback zoom to check sharp-

ness in some cameras). As a result, you will probably waste several sheets of paper while you fine-tune the images to match the output quality you can obtain when printing through a computer.

2. Few direct printers provide controls for adjusting image parameters like brightness, contrast, colour balance and sharpness and, because of factors outlined above, it is impossible to carry out such adjustments on a small screen.

3. Many direct printers will only print JPEG files, which means those who prefer to shoot in RAW or TIFF format must always print via a computer.

The arrival of direct printing systems like PictBridge has had no impact on the overall cost of printing digital photos at home because the equipment and materials used for home-based printing are essentially the same. However, the overall cost of printers has declined slowly in recent years and under-A$200 photo printers are now available, making home-based printing an option for most consumers.

Calculating printing costs

It is difficult to calculate the exact cost of producing an inkjet print because the amount of ink used varies according to the subject of the photograph (prints with strong, dark or highly saturated colours use more ink than misty scenes). Printers with individually replaceable ink cartridges provide greater economy because you replace each ink as it runs out instead of replacing all the inks when the first one is exhausted. This makes precise calculation of ink usage almost impossible. In addition, paper costs can vary according to the weight and surface finish of the paper, the size of each sheet and the number of sheets in the pack. However, we can provide a general guide for inkjet prints, based on 18 months of printer tests, allowing for 10% wastage (due to paper misfeeds, incorrect settings and other such mishaps).

Most photo inkjet printers will produce between 36 and 44 full-bleed A4-sized prints before the first ink runs out. In a typical six-colour ink set, the first colours to be used up are the light ('photo') cyan and magenta inks, closely followed by the yellow ink. So, from a practical viewpoint, users need to replace half of the inks at around the same time. We have used this information to estimate the approximate ink cost per A4 print as the total cost of the ink set divided by 40. This averages out at between A$3 and A$4 per print. Paper costs range from A$1.50 to A$2.50 per sheet for glossy photo weight paper, which means the average cost for a home printed A4 digital photo is between A$5 and A$7, allowing for up to 15% wastage. This is cheaper than the A$12 or more charged by most photolabs.

However, the situation is slightly different for 10 cm x 15 cm snapshot prints. Although snapshot-sized inkjet prints can be produced by most A4 inkjet printers (and a few smaller models), the majority of snapshot printers use thermal dye-based printing technology. With an inkjet printer, the cost per print can be as low as 35 cents or as high as 80 cents, depending on the type of paper used and the way the printer operates. Printers that use three-colour ink sets and package the ink and paper together are the cheapest to run. Although prints from thermal printers are almost indistinguishable from prints from a photolab, the cost per print is between A$1.00 and A$1.50, which is significantly higher than lab prints.

Research in Australia and overseas has shown that consumers tend to use a mixture of home- and lab-based printing for snapshot prints, choosing the former at times when prints are needed straight away or when the lab is closed, and the latter when it is easy to place an order while they shop. However, for enlargements, many more digital photographers are starting to print at home because of the clear cost advantages and the increasing ease with which good photo prints can be obtained from photo inkjet printers.

Inkjet Printer Types

Two types of inkjet printers are available, each requiring a different type of ink. For consumers, the differences are mainly academic as there is no quantifiable difference between the two types in the pricing of similar printers. However, on-going maintenance costs can be higher for one type so it is helpful to understand the differences as they can influence your choice when purchasing a printer.

The majority of inkjet printers use heat to produce bubbles of ink that are forced out through ultra-fine nozzles onto the paper. Canon was the first with this technology and has adopted the name 'Bubble Jet' for its inkjet printers. Printers of this type require inks and print heads that can withstand repeated heating and cooling. This can be an Achilles' heel because repeated heating and cooling can degrade the print heads, so they require periodic replacing. On the plus side, however, thermal inkjets can be very fast. They also produce very tiny dots and deliver a very smooth-looking print.

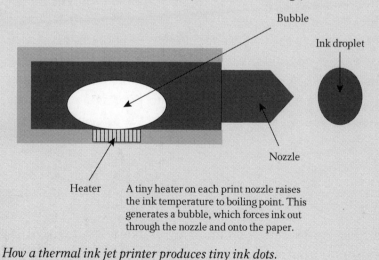

Bubble

Ink droplet

Nozzle

Heater

A tiny heater on each print nozzle raises the ink temperature to boiling point. This generates a bubble, which forces ink out through the nozzle and onto the paper.

How a thermal ink jet printer produces tiny ink dots.

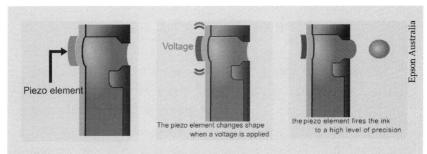

Piezo element

Voltage

The piezo element changes shape when a voltage is applied

the piezo element fires the ink to a high level of precision

Epson Australia

How a piezo-electric printer produces tiny ink dots.

The other inkjet printer type uses piezo-electric technology that causes crystals in the print head to flex, regulating the size of the dots they produce. The ink is not heated during this process and control of droplet sizes is dependent on the electronics that adjust the piezo-electric crystals and the viscosity of the ink. Piezo-electric printers are usually slower than thermal printers but the print heads are more durable and prints from the latest photo printers are at least as good as those from thermal inkjets. Epson is the only manufacturer with inkjet printers using this technology.

Note: it is usually best to stick with the printer manufacturer's inks as third-party inks may not match the viscosity or have the heat tolerance required by the print head. In such cases, the print head will be damaged and replacements can be costly. Cheaper inks are often less colour accurate than inks that have been developed for photo printing and you may waste more money in the long run than paying a slightly higher price for the printer manufacturer's inks.

Buying a printer

The first consideration for most printer buyers is the printer's maximum output size. The majority of snap shooters will find standard 10 cm x 15 cm prints suit most of their day-to-day needs and, when enlargements are required, some may prefer to have them done by a specialist photolab. These buyers will find one of the compact thermal dye-based printers or a snapshot inkjet printer like Epson's PictureMate meet their requirements. For those photographers with 4-megapixel resolution (or higher) cameras who sometimes want to enlarge certain pictures and frame them, an A4 inkjet printer is ideal. Most models can handle both 10 cm x 15 cm and A4 papers (plus a few intermediate sizes) giving users some choice. A few A4 printers (mostly Epson-branded) can accept paper in roll form, allowing users to print out panorama pictures at widths of up to 21 cm. Serious enthusiasts who want large prints for framing will find an A3+ printer ideal. Not only can such printers output to 329 mm x 483 mm paper, they can also produce A4, A5 and sometimes snapshot-sized prints.

Having determined the appropriate output size, buyers should next consider performance. Unfortunately, inkjet printer performance is quite varied: some produce prints that are as good as, and sometimes better than, photographic prints while others produce prints with a limited colour gamut and obvious surface discontinuities. Price is usually a good guide to performance and 'photo' printers tend to produce better results than printers designed for general office use. Although many recently released printers can produce excellent results with minimal adjustments, the more sophisticated models need to be properly set up and integrated into your computer's workflow.

Consumers shopping for a printer should always ask to see sample prints made by the models under consideration. Note that these prints usually represent the best output you can expect from that particular printer and should only be used as a guide to the best quality that printer can deliver. For a more realistic indication of actual performance, take one of your own digital snapshots to the store on a CD or memory card and ask for it to be printed. Look closely at the print to see whether the ink has been laid down smoothly. There should be no visible dot pattern and no evidence of scan lines; colour and tonal gradations should be smooth and continuous and edges should look sharp. Then check the image for colour fidelity and compare its tonal range to the original shot.

When you have found a printer that meets your requirements, check that it comes with everything you need for producing prints. Some printers are not supplied with USB cables, while others come without paper, or with a very small 'sample' pack of paper that runs out quickly. Most inkjet printers are supplied with a full set of inks but some thermal printers come with a sample ink/ribbon pack that can produce only 10 prints. Batteries (and chargers) are usually supplied with portable printers that require them. You can find more information on buying a printer on the *CHOICE* website at www.choice.com.au.

Printer connections

For the past few years, all new printers released to the market have used USB cables as their main connection to a computer and, recently, to digital cameras and some camcorders. USB stands for Universal Serial Bus and is distinguished from the earlier parallel and serial connectors by its 'plug and play' facility. You don't need to turn your computer off to connect a USB device, simply plug it in and switch it on. Most computers sold today come with four or more USB ports, allowing users to connect printers, scanners digital cameras and other devices at will.

USB comes in several 'flavours'. The original USB (designated '1.1') carries data at the rate of 12 megabits per second. This is fast enough for what the standard defines as 'medium to low-speed peripherals', such as digital cameras, modems, keyboards, mice, digital joysticks, some CD-ROM drives, tape and floppy drives and consumer-level scanners and specialty printers. USB 2.0 (also known as 'HiSpeed USB') is four times faster than USB 1.1 (480 Mbits/second) and has been developed for applications that require high data transmission speeds. Currently found in many high-end scanners, DSCs and digital camcorders as well as CD/DVD and optical drives, it is likely to become the standard for digital cameras and printers as well as hubs and other storage devices as sensor resolutions increase and the demand for rapid data transmission grows. An increasing number of new PCs are USB 2.0 enabled but it is easy to add USB 2.0 support to older computers. Note: if you connect a USB 2.0 device to a computer that only supports USB 1.1, it will run at the slower USB 1.1 speed.

Owners of Apple Macintosh computers will find an additional type of connection: FireWire (also known as IEEE-1394, with reference to its international standard definition), which carries data at a rate of 100–400Mbits/second. FireWire is seldom used for printer connections but is popular on digital camcorders as it allows video clips to be downloaded to computers much faster than USB 1.1.

Shooting pictures for printing

Regardless of whether you plan to print your digital photos at home or at a lab, the more image pixels you start with, the better your chance of getting a print that looks 'photographic' and the larger you can make it. This means shooting at the highest available resolution *and* quality settings. Recently, a group of international publishers drew up guidelines covering the optimum print sizes for different image resolution levels as a guide for photographers who wish to submit images for publication in digital form. The resulting table, which has been adapted to provide metric measurements and is reproduced on page 154, provides a useful estimate of the recommended maximum print size from standard cameras under optimum conditions.

If you rely on these guidelines, the only additional adjustment that may need to be made is to resize the images for printing. This may not be necessary as many printers will set the optimum output

Camera/scanner pixel resolution (horizontal x vertical)	Camera sensor resolution (effective megapixels)	Uncompressed file size	Compressed file size (maximum compression allowable)	Maximum print size in centimetres
4500 x 3000	13.5	38.32 MB	1.67 MB	38.1 x 25.4
4064 x 2704	11.0	31.20 MB	1.36 MB	34.29 x 22.86
3008 x 2000	6.0	17.08 MB	0.74 MB	25.4 x 17.02
2560 x 1950	5.0	14.17 MB	0.62 MB	21.59 x 16.51
2448 x 1632	4.0	11.34 MB	0.49 MB	20.83 x 13.72
2000 x 1500	3.0	8.52 MB	0.37 MB	17.02 x 12.70
1600 x 1200	1.9	5.45 MB	0.24 MB	13.46 x 10.16
1280 x 1240	1.3	3.72 MB	0.16 MB	10.92 x 8.64
640 x 480	0.3	0.87 MB	0.04 MB	5.33 x 4.06

Source: *Advanced Digital Photography*, Media Publishing 2004.
www.photoreview.com.au

resolution automatically. However, if you would like an exact guide to the optimum output size for any of your digital photos, you can use the 'Resize Image' control in your editing software to determine it.

Resizing images for printing

For prints up to A4 size, the best resolution setting is 300 ppi (pixels per inch). This can be reduced to 200 ppi for A3-sized prints as the viewing distance is usually great enough to make possible pixelation invisible. Although the location of the image sizing/resizing control varies from one software application to another, the overall principle remains the same. The illustrations below show how to resize an image using Adobe's Photoshop Elements, one of the most popular under-A$200 applications.

The dialog box above shows an image file from a 6-megapixel digital camera. Note the pixel dimensions and document size

Input file dimensions

Output file dimensions

Resolution set by camera

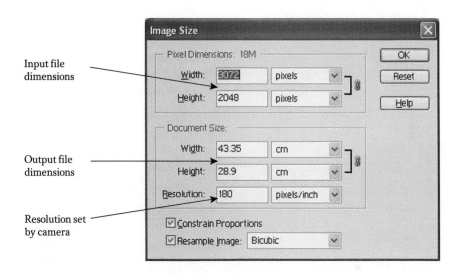

boxes are linked to preserve the aspect ratio. Unchecking the Constrain Proportions box allows these parameters to be adjusted separately.

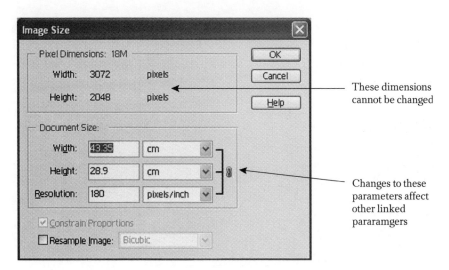

These dimensions cannot be changed

Changes to these parameters affect other linked pararamgers

Unchecking the Resample Image box preserves the Pixel Dimensions, allowing changes to be made to the Width and Height of the output document or the output Resolution.

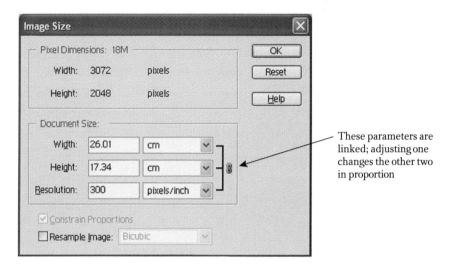

These parameters are linked; adjusting one changes the other two in proportion

Note that when the Resolution is changed to 300 pixels/inch, the Width and Height of the document (print) change accordingly. These figures represent the maximum recommended print size for this image file.

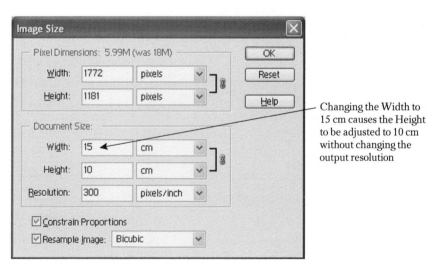

Changing the Width to 15 cm causes the Height to be adjusted to 10 cm without changing the output resolution

To make a smaller print, recheck the Resample image box to preserve the output Resolution then change either the Width or Height dimensions in the Document Size parameters.

Print durability

It will probably surprise some readers to learn that few colour photos maintain their original colours and contrast range for more than 20 years and, indeed, some may change in as little as a couple of months. All types of prints are affected, as are colour films, both negative and slide. The reason is that the dyes used for film-based photography and most types of printing are inherently unstable. All colour prints can be affected by environmental factors like light, heat, humidity, air quality and physical handling, but some of these factors have a greater impact on different types of prints.

Traditional photo prints are vulnerable to ultraviolet light as well as airborne gases, while inkjet prints are most affected by atmospheric pollutants (especially ozone) and humidity. (It's ironic that so many people display photo prints on the refrigerator door or in rooms with home entertainment equipment and/or air conditioners as all these devices are sources of ozone and tend to accelerate the rates at which colours in prints are lost.)

A great deal of research has been done over the past 25 years on the 'light-fastness' of both traditional and inkjet media and measurements are now available to show how long particular media can be displayed in standard room conditions before visible colour changes occur. The table on page 158 shows some typical light-fastness ratings for a range of popular printing media, when prints are displayed unprotected by glass or plastic lamination (both of which provide significant protection against all types of discolouration).

Readers will note that the longest lifetimes come from prints made on photo quality inkjet paper with pigment-based inks. The reason these prints are so much more durable than prints made with dye-based inks is that dyes are dissolved in the ink itself and, when applied to the paper they become dispersed in the image-forming layer. In contrast, pigment inks consist of tiny insoluble particles of solid colour. Although usually larger than the ink molecules, they

Media	Estimated time to show visible colour changes in normal display conditions (without protection)
Photographic colour printing paper	11.5–15.3 years (standard photolab papers) 15.8–60 years (professional papers)
Photo quality inkjet paper plus dye-based inks	< 0.5 years to >20 years
Photo quality inkjet paper plus pigment-based inks	> 100 years
Thermal dye transfer prints	1.5–7.3 years

Note: The table above is based on data from Wilhelm Imaging Research, Inc. which specialises in image permanence. Details can be found at www.wilhelm-research.com.

have certain advantages for photo printing. They are much more resistant to all kinds of fading and they do not drift when applied to the paper. Both dyes and pigments are dispersed in a liquid, which evaporates as the print dries. But dyes are much more vulnerable to attack by ozone than pigments and some pigment ink manufacturers coat their pigment particles with resin to provide additional protection against pollutants, hence their higher longevity.

If you want prints to last for the maximum amount of time, look for acid-free papers with 'archival' qualities and use a printer that uses pigment-based inks. Allow each print to dry for a minute or so as it comes out of the printer before handling it and then cover each print with a sheet of plain paper and leave it to 'cure' for at least 24 hours before mounting it for display or storing it in an album. Then protect your prints against environmental contaminants by either encapsulating them in plastic (laminating) or framing them behind glass. Currently, the longest lasting inkjet prints come from certain Epson printers that use pigment-based inks. When these are combined with Epson's Archival Matte paper, prints with lifetimes in excess of 100 years can be produced.

Transferring Pictures to a Computer

If your computer is running one of the latest operating systems (Windows or Mac), transferring digital photos from the camera is easy and, if the camera supports PTP (Picture Transfer Protocol) as many recent models do, you may not need to load driver software. You can connect the camera directly, using the supplied USB cable or remove the memory card and slot it into a tethered card reader.

To transfer images via a **USB cable**:

1. If your camera isn't PTP-enabled, load the driver software onto your PC.
2. Plug the USB cable into the computer and connect the camera.
3. If the camera is plug-and-play, a dialogue box should appear on the screen after a couple of seconds, giving you a choice of things to do with the image files (for example viewing or transferring). If the screen doesn't appear, click on Start>Control Panel>Hardware>Scanners and Cameras and then right-click on the camera you are using.
4. Follow the on-screen instructions.

To transfer images via a **card reader**:

1. Make sure the camera has finished writing the image files and switch it off.
2. Plug the USB cable from the card reader into the computer.
3. Remove the card from the camera and insert it in the relevant slot on the card reader. Make sure it's the right way round (if it doesn't slip in easily, it is incorrectly orientated).
4. Follow the instructions that appear in the dialog box.

Note: You may need to set up a special folder for your photos before transferring the image files, although some cameras will do this for you using the date as the folder's name. Most PCs let you choose between Copying the image files, which leaves the originals on the memory card so you can take it to a photolab if you want prints made of some pictures, or Moving the image files, which leaves no images on the memory card. When you have transferred all the files, you should 'Safely Remove' the device from the computer before extracting the card.

Organising image files

In the old days, it was traditional to store prints in shoeboxes, after first separating the best pictures out for mounting in albums or frames. Today, however, digital images can be stored in several ways. All have advantages and disadvantages.

Keeping your digital photos on your computer's hard disk drive (HDD) may be fine when you first start taking digital pictures but, before long, the HDD will fill up and you'll have to find another storage solution. Many people archive folders of image files to CD (or more recently, DVD) and this can be a good solution provided some cautions are observed.

1. Use high-quality disks that are rated for longevity as cheap disks can deteriorate in as little as six months and your photographs may become inaccessible.
2. Make at least two copies of each set of photos. Keep one near your computer so you can access them regularly and store the other off-site in a security box or similar facility. This ensures that if something disastrous happens at home, another copy of each picture is still preserved.
3. 'Migrate' all image files to a new disk roughly once a year to ensure they retain their integrity. Recent tests in Europe have

shown that optical disks may not live up to their 'archival' claims. Check your files every six months or so to see whether any deterioration has occurred (if it's difficult to access them, use a data rescue program open them and resave them on new media).

A number of under-A$100 image data management applications are available to help you keep track of image files. The problem with all of them is that you have to tag and organise the images as you download them for storage so, if you already have lots of digital images stored in different folders on your PC, this sort of program may not meet your needs as you will need to open each folder and tag images individually.

The first image management application for consumers was Adobe's Photoshop Album (RRP A$169) but several other manufacturers have similar applications. Corel's Photobook which sells for less than A$70 and Jasc's Paint Shop Photo Album 5 (RRP $US45) are both keenly priced and easy to use. All three applications are suitable for in use Windows only. Details are available at www.adobe.com, www.corel.com and www.jasc.com.

Interesting Fact #11

Consumers buying inkjet papers need to be aware that different manufacturers use different ways to measure print longevity. Most manufacturers base their claims on tests conducted by Wilhelm Imaging Research, which exposes prints to standard lab-filtered cool-white fluorescent lighting, extrapolated to an exposure equivalent to 12 hours per day at a brightness level of 450 lux. Tests are conducted in rooms held at 75° Fahrenheit (24 °C) and 60% humidity.

Kodak's tests on print media also involve 12 hours of light exposure per day but the intensity of the light is 120 lux. The

---

company claims this light level is 'a good overall estimate for typical home conditions'. It also states that the 'recommended range of temperature and humidity for print display is 68–77°F (20–25°C) and 40–60% relative humidity, which is much wider than the range used in Wilhelm Research's tests. Kodak also claims that "glass-filtered fluorescent lights may contain a higher level of ultraviolet light than is typically found in the home or office" and says that the lights should be filtered with Plexiglass instead. They also claim "air quality is not usually a concern in the home", whereas Wilhelm says: "Commonly encountered 'worst case' not 'average' display and storage conditions found in homes and offices in locations throughout the world must be taken into account both in the test methods themselves and in reporting test results."

Not surprisingly, inkjet media manufacturers who rely on Wilhelm Research's testing say consumers may be misled into thinking prints on Kodak media will last longer than those on other manufacturers' products, simply on the basis of the numbers alone.

More information can be found at
www.wilhelm-research.com and
http://www.kodak.com/US/en/corp/researchDevelopment/.

Chapter 12

Editing digital images

Most photographers like to improve the shots from their cameras with editing software and many affordable packages are now available with functions to suit all levels of expertise from raw amateur to serious professional. All applications support the following editing processes: resizing and cropping, rotating images so they are viewed the right way up, brightness, colour and contrast adjustments, and correction of red-eye in flash shots.

Basic editing software

For some digital photographers, all the necessary tools are available in the software supplied with their computer. Apple's iPhoto provides brightness and contrast adjustments, cropping and resizing facilities, red-eye removal, monochrome conversion, automatic colour correction and a blemish removal tool. Windows XP includes Microsoft Photo Editor, a surprisingly versatile application with three editing menus. The Image menu supports cropping, resizing, rotation, balance (brightness, contrast and gamma adjustment) and auto balance (which is similar to an auto levels control). The Effects menu has tools for sharpening, softening, positive/negative conversion and despeckling (noise reduction) plus edges, chalk and charcoal, emboss, graphic pen, notepaper, watercolour, stained glass, stamp and texturiser tools. The Tools menu has smudge, sharpen and set transparent colour tools. These built-in editors give you a good starting point, but their functionality is limited and most photographers require more powerful applications.

The following under-A$300 packages are ideal for beginners:

- ACDSee FotoCanvas is a dedicated editing application with tools for enhancing and correcting digital images. It includes a handy image browser, text and graphics tools and 40 digital filters. Visit www.acdsystems.com for more information.
- Adobe Photoshop Album is more of an image organising tool than an editing tool. Editing facilities include cropping, red-eye removal and brightness and contrast adjustment (Windows only). Visit www.adobe.com.au for more information.
- ArcSoft PhotoImpression 5 has a customisable user interface, lots of project wizards and automatic enhancement and correction facilities. The bundled clip art includes templates and frames as well as file organisation and printing controls. Visit www.arcsoft.com for more information.
- Corel Photobook combines image management and sharing facilities with the most commonly used editing functions. Printing support includes the ability to print multiple images on one sheet of paper (Windows only). Visit www.corel.com for more information.
- Jasc Paint Shop Photo Album 5 is wizard-based and includes image editing, cropping, stitching and edging functions plus file management facilities. You can also resize images for emailing and create video CD slide shows (Windows only). Visit www.jasc.com for more information.
- Microsoft Digital Image Suite 9 uses wizards and templates to provide users with simple ways to perform common tasks. Hundreds of design templates are provided for creating image-based projects for home and business users (Windows only). Go to www.microsoft.com for more information.

The following under-A\$300 packages will suit digital photographers with some computer experience and photographic knowledge:

- Adobe Photoshop Elements 3.0 is built around the core structure of Adobe's professional Photoshop application and offers a wide range of photo editing, processing and enhancement tools. The feature set is smaller and the price is substantially lower but many functions in the two programs are identical or very similar. RRP around A\$179. Visit www.adobe.com.au for more information.
- Jasc Paint Shop Pro 9 combines photo editing with graphic design. It offers more flexibility than Photoshop Elements and includes draw and paint tools, hundreds of special effects, distortion tools, animation facilities and perspective corrections. Visit www.jasc.com for more information.
- Microsoft Digital Image Pro 9 is the simplest of the packages in this category to use, thanks to its wizard- and template-based structure. It has a wider range of tools than Digital Image Suite 9 but a similar overall structure. (Windows only) Go to www.microsoft.com for more information.
- Ulead PhotoImpact XL combines a full set of editing tools with painting and drawing facilities. Wizard-based assistance is provided, along with image management facilities, digital effects, 2-D and 3-D graphics creation, text annotation and Web graphics as well as image sharing. Visit www.ulead.com for more information.

Many popular image editors are offered as either freeware (no cost) or shareware applications (downloadable trial versions). With shareware, the program will work normally for the trial period, after which you have to pay if you want to use it. (Shareware prices normally range from about A\$35 to \$120.) The following programs are worth a look:

- The GIMP (GNU Image Manipulation Program) is a popular freeware application that includes photo retouching, image composition and image authoring. It was first developed for UNIX but also works with Linux operating systems and has also been released for Mac and Windows PCs. Go to www.gimp.org.
- DCEnhancer is another freeware image editor. As well as standard retouching tools it includes noise reduction, tonal balancing and colour correction. It can be found at www.media chance.com.
- Serif Software's PhotoPlus 5.5 is a Windows only freeware application that includes basic photo editing facilities, support for TWAIN scanners and cameras and a full range of export options (including Web graphics). It can be downloaded from www.freeserifsoftware.com.
- Irfanview is a small, fast graphics viewer with basic editing facilities (cropping, effects, sharpening), slideshow support, lossless JPEG rotation and many plug-ins. It's Windows only and can be found at www.irfanview.com.
- VCW VicMan's Photo Editor is a versatile image editor that includes image editing tools, filters and effects. A basic version is available as freeware, while a more powerful 'Pro' version costs $US29.95 to download. Go to www.vicman.net.
- JPhotoBrush Pro is a multi-platform image editing/enhance-ment/retouching application that sells for around A$35. It has a user-friendly interface and provides plenty of effects and filters. Available from www.jphotobrushpro.com.
- PhotoLine 32 a German-developed image editor for Windows and Mac operating systems. It costs €59 to download and 30-day trial versions are available from www.pl32.com.
- FxFoto 2.0 is a suite of software tools for organising, editing and sharing photos that is available in three versions. FxFoto 2.0 Standard is a fully functional free download, while the Deluxe Collage Edition (which adds multi-photo collages, scrapbook-ing, multimedia slide shows and photo stitching) can be

obtained for $US29.99 and Pro Media Edition (which adds photo-based movies and the ability to publish non-editable content) for $US39.99. All titles are upgradeable. Go to www.triscape.com.

Some easy video editing applications that can be used to assemble movies from clips captured by DSCs include:

- Apple iMovie is ideal for editing DSC video clips and will suit beginners with its simple user interface plus abundant features and special effects. Users who want to record their movies on DVD can combine it with Apple's iDVD (Mac only). Details can be found at www.apple.com.
- Pinnacle Studio 9 combines video and audio editing tools with some special effects and excellent titling facilities. It can also be used for DVD authoring. Product details and a 30-day trial download are available at www.pinnaclesys.com.
- Screenblast Movie Studio is wizard-based and allows users to combine stills with video clips and output the end result to DVD or Video CD. It also supports a 'blue screen' effect that lets users insert different images and backgrounds into video clips. Go to www.screenblast.com.
- Ulead VideoStudio 8 costs more than the above packages but is significantly more powerful and versatile. Its large preview window and extensive capture and import facilities make it a fast, efficient and highly usable video editor. Trial downloads can be found at www.ulead.com.

Common editing tasks

Before embarking on any editing process that will alter an image in any way, always archive the image at its original capture resolution and in its original file format. This is done by transferring the image data straight from the camera to your PC or to a CD-ROM or other storage device *without changing it in any way*. This file is kept as your master image and should only be opened when you need to make a copy to work on. If the original image is a JPEG file, you should also archive an extra back-up copy as TIFF image file or in the uncompressed file format supported by your editing software. This back-up copy will be the one you go to when you want a copy of the image to work on. The reason for this strategy is simple: if you make a mistake during the editing process you will always have an unaltered version of the image you captured to return to.

The most frequently used editing procedures are:

- changing the size, shape, orientation and file format of a picture
- adjusting brightness, contrast, colour saturation and colour mode (black-and-white or sepia)
- correcting red eyes in flash shots
- adding text and graphics to pictures
- copying, cutting and pasting operations on part or all of the image. We will look at some of these in more detail.

Resizing still images

Resizing is used for two main purposes: to reduce the size of image files for emailing or posting on websites or to produce files that are the correct size for printing. The latter topic was covered in Chapter 11 so we will focus here on resizing pictures for emailing.

Pictures destined for emailing should always be converted into JPEG (*.jpg) files because JPEGs can be viewed in all popular web browsers and used with e-mail software. Many software packages include an automatic facility (sometimes tagged 'Save for Web') that automatically produces a small copy of the image file that will transmit and download quickly.

Some digital cameras can produce small, low-resolution copies of shots, either automatically or if you press a 'small pic' or 'email' button. Other cameras allow you to do this via a dedicated 'share' button on the camera that opens an email application when you connect the camera to your computer, either via a USB cable or by slipping it into a docking station. In most cases, the designated file

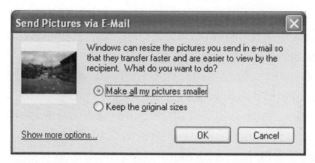

Some applications include an auto resizing function that works on a batch of image files.

is sent as an attachment, after being automatically resized (if necessary).

All images that will be emailed or used in Web pages should be resized to a resolution of 72 pixels/inch (this is the default setting on many digital cameras) and the image size should be no larger than 1024 x 768 pixels because that is the display limit of most monitors. Save the file as a copy (using the tag 'for email' makes it easily recognisable if you want to resend it at any time) and use the JPEG compression menu (which usually pops up automatically when you select 'save as') to reduce the file size.

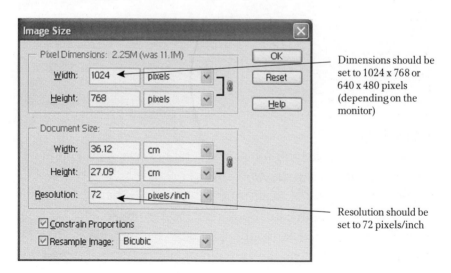

Dimensions should be set to 1024 x 768 or 640 x 480 pixels (depending on the monitor)

Resolution should be set to 72 pixels/inch

Most shots can be reduced to less than 100 KB without obvious quality loss when displayed on a computer screen. Many editing programs display how long the file will take to send at the selected resolution and you can usually select from several modem speeds (broadband and dial-up options are covered). Using this as a guide, adjust the compression level to ensure each file takes only a few seconds to transmit. (It's well worth having software with this facility as it will save you money in Internet costs and minimise frustration when your files download quickly to the recipient's PC.)

Emailed images are best sent as attachments; simply write your message and click on the attachment icon (normally represented by a paper clip). This will take you into the file browser; locate the file and click on 'attach'(or Insert, OK or Open) and it's ready to send. If you plan to send several shots together, keep the total for each email under 1 MB to ensure it gets through. (Many ISPs restrict the amount of data a recipient can receive.)

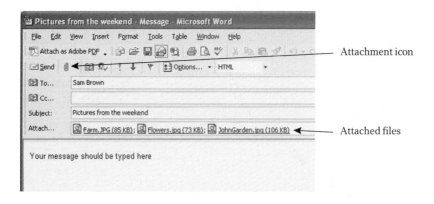

Attachment icon

Attached files

Cropping

Images may require cropping for several reasons, most commonly to exclude unwanted elements in the picture and to change the aspect ratio of the shot so it fits better on printing paper. The same tool is used in both situations and most software applications provide at least a basic cropping facility. The process is straight-forward: simply select the cropping tool and drag it across the image to define the area you want to crop out. Most applications 'grey out' the remainder of the picture and many let users adjust the boundaries of the area to be cropped before finalising the procedure. A step-by-step guide to cropping is provided below.

The original photograph has distracting background details that take the viewer's attention away from the main subjects.

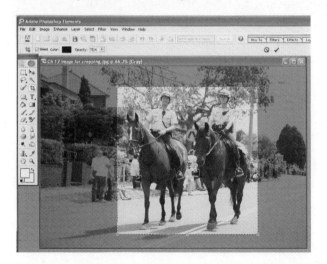

Use the cropping tool to select the main subject you wish to retain. Note the greying out of the parts of the image that will be discarded. The borders of the cropped area can be adjusted by clicking on the edge or corner of the cropped area and dragging it in or out.

171

Selecting Image>Crop discards the unwanted area, leaving the cropped picture. Note the aspect ratio has been changed quite dramatically by this process.

Brightness, colour and contrast correction

Software applications differ quite widely in the types of colour adjustment they provide and the extent to which you can vary the colour settings. There are three main types of colour controls: ring-around displays, eyedropper selectors and sliders. Examples are shown on page 4 of the colour insert

Colour ring-arounds are simple to use and quite intuitive, although some applications lack slider controls for fine-tuning adjustments and, in many, the thumbnail images are too small to let you see the full effects of the selected adjustment. With a few applications, you can choose whether the adjustment will be applied to the midtones, shadows or highlights and control colour saturation. You can also control the degree of adjustment with a slider control, giving you a vast range of options to explore.

Eyedropper systems let you set a 'neutral grey' point by clicking on an eyedropper icon and positioning it on an area in the image that should be white, black or grey. All image colours will then be adjusted to be in balance with that neutral reference and should, in theory, be correct. Unfortunately, the system doesn't always work as it should because some image files don't have a suitable reference area within them. Users also vary in their ability to determine what is the best part of the image to use as a reference point. Expertise is developed with experience. When it works, the eyedropper system delivers good results and is very easy to use. When it doesn't, you can usually go back and try again until you achieve a suitable outcome.

Most high-end and many mid-level editing applications provide slider adjustments for colour and brightness control, and some also include a slider for adjusting saturation. These controls should be used with great care. Slider control accuracy depends on the length of the adjustment and the degree of change permitted by the software. The long sliders found in high-end applications generally support more fine-tuning than short ones, which are common in entry- and mid-level applications. These packages may also allow users to adjust each colour channel individually via an 'Edit' dropdown menu.

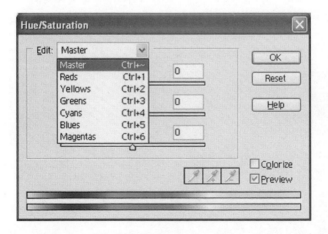

The slider controls in Photoshop Elements 3.0 for Hue and Saturation have a dropdown Edit menu that allows users to fine-tune each colour channel individually.

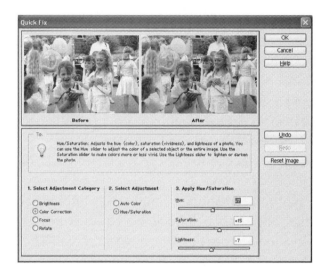

Applications that provide a real-time preview that shows you the effect of any adjustment make editing easier.

Best results are obtained when you can see the changes applied to the image via a Preview facility so you know how far to move the slider. Always check modifications by enlarging critical sections of the image before committing to any change. Fortunately, if you apply the wrong adjustment, most software allows you to go back

More powerful software applications, such as Adobe Photoshop, provide a wider range of tonal adjustments than entry-level packages.

and undo the effect, provided you do so immediately without making any other changes to the image file.

The ability to adjust highlights, shadows and midtones individually or apply different adjustments to individual colour channels is well worth looking for when you're buying an image editing application. Using these settings is often the best way to achieve the desired result.

Producing panoramas

One of the more interesting things you can do with a digital camera is to capture a sequence of shots and 'stitch' them together to produce a panoramic image. Many DSCs include a panorama setting that will display the last shot taken to provide a reference image against which the next shot can be positioned. While this function works well, it can be difficult to see the reference image clearly enough to use it in bright outdoor lighting. (This is one situation where DSCs with EVFs have a significant advantage.)

With practice, anyone can learn to capture a sequence of 'stitchable' shots. The procedure is straightforward:

1. Stand on a spot that lets you capture the field of view without moving your feet. It is important to keep this position throughout the shooting sequence. Any change in position means a corresponding change in the perspective of the shots. If this happens, the shots will not stitch together correctly.
2. Take the sequence of shots, moving from left to right (or bottom to top) swivelling at the waist and overlapping adjacent shots by between 30% and 50%. Do not change your position or any of the camera's settings at any point in the shooting sequence.

When the image files are uploaded to the computer, special software is required to stitch them together. In cameras with a 'panorama assist' function, this software is usually supplied. For cameras without panorama assist, a good freeware/shareware application is Panorama Factory, which can be downloaded from www.panoramafactory.com. Some general-purpose editing applications (such as Adobe's Photoshop Elements, Jasc Paint Shop Pro and Ulead PhotoImpact) include panorama stitching (or 'photo merge') controls. These vary in facility and may work better with some types of subjects than with others.

Import the images into the application and follow the on-screen instructions (these vary from one program to another). Few panoramas stitch together perfectly so you will probably need to make some minor adjustments to obtain a satisfactory result. Some programs let you move adjacent images manually to produce a better 'stitch'. In other cases, you may need to save the stitched image and then import it into a general editing program, where you can touch up joins that remain visible. Use the cloning or 'healing' tool and work on an enlarged view of the area. Illustrations showing how to create a panorama can be found on pages 6 and 7 of the colour inset.

Interesting Fact #12

Although you can do a lot with editing software, there are some problems that cannot be corrected. The most common of them are:

1. Shooting with the resolution and quality settings too low. Although most editing software lets you increase file sizes by interpolation (adding pixels on the basis of existing pixels in the area), the more pixels that are added by upsampling, the greater the loss of image quality. Always shoot with the highest resolution and quality settings; little quality is lost when you downsample image files.

2. Gross over- or under-exposure (including shots of strongly backlit subjects without flash fill). You can't add pictorial information that wasn't captured by the camera.

3. Some colour casts cannot be removed, including the imbalance that occurs with mixed lighting. For example, if your subject is partly lit by daylight and partly by artificial light, the auto white balance will produce a shot in which the areas lit by daylight look pinkish, while those lit by artificial light could appear greenish or orange. You can usually adjust the colour balance to minimise one colour cast but not both.

4. Out-of-focus shots should generally be classed as unusable, although the sharpening control can improve shots that are only slightly blurred, as long as sharpening is not excessive and the resulting images are kept small (snapshot-sized prints or smaller).

Digital imaging glossary

Achromatic lenses contain different types of glass that correct the focus at the blue and red ends of the spectrum, pulling them in to focus near the green focus point.

Adaptive signal processing (ASP): A mathematical processing system that uses feedback and predictive techniques to ensure digitised signals (and hence, digital photos) are produced with high levels of accuracy and low noise levels.

Additive colours (primaries): The three primary colours of light—red, green and blue. These are used by digital cameras, monitors and scanners to produce colour images. When all three are added in equal quantities, the result is white light.

Advanced photo system (APS): The APS film format was introduced about 12 years ago to simplify film loading and act as a 'bridge' from conventional film to digital but it has not met with great popularity. Although the cameras were attractive (being smaller than their 35mm equivalents) the format was too small to produce good quality pictures so most manufacturers have stopped making them. Canon still makes one or two models and all film manufacturers have APS single-use cameras in their range.

AF assist: A special light on the DSC's body that is used to illuminate the subject in low light, improving focusing accuracy. Its range is normally limited to around four metres so it is only effective for close subjects. Some DSCs use infrared light while others use visible light. In the latter cameras, the light may double as a red-eye reduction lamp.

Aliasing: (also known as 'jaggies') The step-like effect that can be seen in digital images when they are enlarged to reveal their pixel structure. Many camera signal processing systems include anti-aliasing software that minimises the effect.

Analogue-to-digital converter (ADC or A/D converter): A device or processor used for converting an analogue signal, such as a voltage level or video signal, into digital data.

Aperture: The adjustable 'pupil' in a camera through which light passes to create the photograph. In most cameras, it consists of overlapping blades which are adjusted by an electrical motor, although in simpler digicams, the aperture may consist of two plates with different-sized holes (or f-stops). The aperture value (f-number) of a lens is the ratio of the focal length of the lens to the diameter of its entrance pupil. The larger the f-number, the smaller the entrance pupil and the less light it allows in.

Apochromatic lenses bring all three wavebands (red, green and blue) to a common focus, minimising fringing effects. A super-achromatic lens corrects for four or more wavelengths and should eliminate all colour errors.

Artefacts: Undesirable visual defects produced by digital imaging systems. They can be generated by either input or output devices and include noise, colour casts, distortions and lost information. All degrade image quality.

Artificial intelligence (Ai): Also known as 'intelligent' (i). A mathematical processing system that fine-tunes information to produce results that are closer to the way human beings see objects. Examples include AiAF for focusing, and iTTL for through-the-lens metering systems.

Aspect ratio: The relationship between the horizontal and vertical dimensions of an image. A 35mm film frame has an aspect ratio of 3:2 (which is the same as a standard 10 cm x 15 cm print). Most compact digital cameras produce images with a 4:3 aspect ratio.

Autofocus (AF): A camera control that focuses the lens on the subject. The two types of AF in common use are infrared (IR) and contrast-based. The former fires a beam of infrared light at the subject and calculates its distance on the basis of the return reflection, while the latter evaluates distance on the basis of image contrast (close subjects have higher contrast than their background). Many DSCs include servo-AF systems that can focus on a moving subject. This is also known as 'focus tracking' and it is normally engaged by switching to a special designated mode (continuous, 'tracking' or 'AI servo').

Audio video interleave (AVI): A video file format that commonly carries one video ('vids') stream and one audio ('auds') stream. Developed by Microsoft, it is the most common format for audio/video data on the PC.

Barrel distortion: A type of image distortion that expands the central dimensions of the picture without affecting the periphery. It is most common in wide-angle lenses.

Batteries: The power source(s) for digital cameras, batteries are important because most digital cameras are power hungry. Many cameras are now supplied with rechargeable batteries, either NiMH or lithium-ion, along with a specially designed charger.

B&W: Popular shorthand for 'black and white', B&W denotes an image that contains only brightness levels. No colour information is recorded. B&W images are also known as 'greyscale' images (see entry).

Bit: Short for 'binary digit', a bit is the smallest piece of information that can be handled by a computer and has a value of 0 or 1.

Bit depth: The number of bits used to specify the brightness (for B&W) or colour range of each pixel in an image sensor. Images that contain 8 bits of information can record 256 tonal gradations. When we speak of 8-bit colour images (which are used by most digital imaging systems), we really mean 8 bits each of blue, green and red data (24 bits in all), which is equivalent to 16.7 million distinct hues and tones. Professional cameras and software—and most scanners—can capture images at higher bit depths (12-bit or 16-bit) but the advantages of this can only be realised in professional software that can handle the additional data. The resulting image files are roughly twice the size of 8-bit files and provide a better platform than 8-bit images for enlargement to A3 size or larger.

Bitmap: A file format that records image data as individual pixels. Denoted by the extension *.bmp.

Blooming: The halo effect that occurs at borders between dark and light image tones due to an overflow of electrical charge that is generated by excessive light exposure on part or all of the image sensor.

Bracketing: A technique whereby a series of images of the same subject are taken using a variety of different settings on either side of a set position. Many cameras support exposure bracketing, while some also provide focus and white balance bracketing. In cameras with auto-bracketing, the camera will capture the set of images automatically, allowing the photographer to choose the one that best matches the subject. This control is handy when lighting varies in intensity and colour.

Buffer memory: A special RAM storage area in a digital camera's memory system where image data is held prior to processing and transfer to the camera's memory card. A large buffer memory is required to support high-speed continuous shooting, especially at high image resolution.

Burst (continuous) shooting: A similar function to motor drive in a film SLR camera which allows the camera to capture a sequence of shots in rapid succession. The number of frames that can be captured depends on the image resolution and the size of the camera's buffer memory.

Byte: A bundle of data containing 8 bits.

Calibration: The process of setting up equipment to ensure a predictable output. This is an essential early step for good colour printing.

Charge-coupled device (CCD): A light-sensitive array of silicon cells that is commonly used for digital camera image sensors. It generates electrical current in proportion to light input and allows the simultaneous capture of many pixels with one brief exposure.

Chroma: The colour information associated with an image.

Cloning: The process of reproducing part or all of a digital image for transfer either to another image file or a different area within the same file.

Complementary metal-oxide semiconductor (CMOS): The alternative sensor array to CCD. CMOS sensors are cheaper to manufacture, use less power and, until recently, have produced lower colour reproduction quality than CCD sensors. However, several manufacturers (notably Canon and Foveon) have recently introduced CMOS sensors for digital cameras that produce high colour quality, marking out CMOS as a technology that can be expected in future digital imaging systems.

CMYK: The basic colours used in four-colour printing. The letters 'C', 'M' and 'Y' stand for the subtractive primary colours cyan, magenta and yellow, while 'K' represents black, which is added to compensate for the lack of purity in C, M and Y inks.

Codec: The coding/decoding system used for video capture. The most commonly used codecs are AVI (see entry), Motion JPEG (see entry) and QuickTime (see entry). All can be read by the latest PC operating systems.

Colour space: A geometric system used to describe a range of colours. Adobe RGB (1998) and sRGB are the most commonly used colour spaces in digital imaging.

Colour filter array: A mask of thin layers of dye applied over a digital camera sensor to enable it to record colour information. The individual colour patches filter out all but the chosen colour for that photosite. Software interpolation is used to create a colour value for the resulting pixel based on surrounding pixel values.

The most common filter pattern is the Bayer array, which is used for two filter types: the primary array, which uses alternating rows of red/green and green/blue patches (GRGB) and the complementary array, which replaces green with its complement, magenta; red with cyan and blue with yellow (MCMY).

Compression: A mathematical processing system used to reduce the size of digital data files. Two types of compression are common in digital imaging: lossy (which sacrifices some data in order to obtain small files) and lossless (which involves little or no information loss).

Continuous tone: Also knows as 'greyscale', this describes a black-and-white image, consisting of a continuous gradient of tones from black to white.

Contrast: The difference between the lightest and darkest tones in an image. High-contrast images contain few steps between the lightest and darkest parts of the image, while low-contrast images contain many tonal gradations.

DCIM (Digital camera image): A root level folder in a digital camera or on a personal computer in which image data from a digital camera is stored. Each time you turn on the camera or insert a different card, any empty folders within the DCIM folder are removed. New folders are created automatically in the computer with each set of image downloads.

Depth-of-field: The range of distances in a photograph that are in acceptably sharp focus. Depth-of-field is regulated by the lens aperture, subject distance and the size of the imaging area (sensor or film frame). It is at its greatest with small lens apertures, distant subjects and small imaging areas. Because compact DSCs have very small sensors, it is difficult to shoot subjects with a narrow depth-of-field.

Digital zoom: A zoom effect created by enlarging the central portion of the image. Most cameras interpolate the captured data up to the selected camera resolution but this involves some loss of image quality.

DPI (dots per inch): The most commonly used unit of measurement for describing the resolution of digital image files for printing or scanning. Closely related to ppi for pixels per inch, which is used more generally for image size and resolution.

Digital print order format (DPOF): Most digital cameras are compatible with the Digital print order format (DPOF), a special type of metadata that lets users specify the photos they want to print by using the camera's menu system. The DPOF file is written to the camera's removable media, from which it can be read and executed by printing services and computer-based applications. Note: although most professional and commercial printing systems are fully DPOF compatible, not all digital printers offer full DPOF support—a point worth checking when buying a digital printer.

Driver: Dedicated software that allows a computer to interface with and control another device, such as a printer or scanner.

Dye sublimation: Also known as 'thermal dye sublimation' or 'dye-sub' this colour printing technology forms images by a diffusion transfer process that transfers gaseous dyes from a donor material to a receiving layer. Heat is required for the process. The output is near photographic in quality.

Dynamic range: The measurable difference between the brightest highlight and darkest shadow area in an image that can be reproduced by an imaging system.

Effective pixels: The number of pixels that are actually used to produce the image (as distinct from the total pixel count for the sensor). The remaining pixels (the difference between total and effective pixels) are used to provide a 'dark current reading' so the camera has a black reference point and some may be covered to allow the camera manufacturer to use a particular lens/body combination or provide a 4:3 aspect ratio for resulting images. The number of unused pixels is at the camera manufacturer's discretion, which is why effective pixel count is the only reliable guide to the camera's resolution potential.

Exchangeable image file (Exif): A metadata format developed by the Japan Electronic Industry Development Association (JEIDA). Exif is a preferred image format for digital cameras in the international standard ISO 12234-1 which covers image storage on removable memory. It is closely associated with JPEG, which means it will be compatible with virtually any device or software application that stores and reads JPEGs.

Exposure value (EV): A number determined by the brightness of the subject and the sensitivity selected for the recording medium, it is larger for bright subjects and smaller for dark ones. When the amount of light striking the CCD doubles, the EV increases by 1, making the value equivalent to one stop of exposure.

File format: The way in which digital information is saved by a software application. The most commonly used file formats for digital imaging are JPEG, TIFF and bitmap (BMP).

Filters: Software tools that are used to change the appearance of digital images by adjusting the values or arrangement of certain pixels.

FireWire: Also known as 'iLINK' or 'IEEE 1394', it is a popular system for connecting peripheral devices to PCs (particularly with Macintosh computers and Sony camcorders). It has the advantage of being faster than USB 1.0, making it useful for video applications.

Gamma: The technical term used to describe image contrast, it refers to the slope of the line that represents image output values versus image input values. It is applicable to both film-based and digital images.

Gamut: The range of colours that an image contains or an output device can reproduce.

Graphics tablet: A peripheral computer device that replaces the mouse with a pen and recording surface which allows users to plot position points with fine control over graphics input.

Greyscale (Grayscale): An image consisting only of brightness information represented by a range of grey tones as opposed to pure black-and-white or colour images. The full range of tones can be captured in only 8 bits, which can be handled by most editing software.

Histogram: A graphical display that shows the distribution of tones within an image. The horizontal co-ordinate represents the possible pixel values from black to white, while the vertical co-ordinate shows the number of pixels in the image at each value.

Horizontal resolution: The number of pixels (for images) or lines (for video) a system can resolve along a horizontal axis.

Inkjet: A type of printer that applies microscopic ink droplets to paper to form images, graphics or text.

Interpolation: A mathematical resampling technique which increases or decreases the size of an image file by creating more pixels on the basis of existing pixel values. Some quality is sacrificed as a result of the interpolation process, particularly if files are made larger through interpolation.

JPEG: The image file format developed by the Joint Photographic Experts Group and denoted by the '.jpg' extension. JPEG uses compression algorithms to reduce file sizes, sacrificing some image data to obtain small files. The latest version, JPEG 2000, has recently been released but is not widely used as yet.

Kelvin (K): The international standard for temperature, based on the colour of light from a heated black body. The lower the colour temperature (and Kelvin value), the redder the light and the higher the colour temperature, the bluer.

Kilobyte (KB): 1024 bytes of computer memory.

Lag: A term denoting delay after an action has been initiated. The most common lag times in digital imaging include shutter lag, auto-focus (AF) lag and processing lag. Shutter lag describes the time taken for the camera to capture the shot after the shutter release has been pressed. AF lag defines the time it takes the camera to autofocus and processing lag describes the time images take to be processed and transferred to the memory card so the next image can be captured. (Processing lag normally only affects cameras with little or no buffer memory.)

Liquid crystal display (LCD): LCD screens are used in digital cameras to preview and review shots. In some cameras they replace the optical viewfinder. Most also provide access to the camera controls via a set of menus, which are called up on screen and selected by pressing a button. Some cameras have separate LCD screens that display status information, such as frame counts, camera settings and battery power.

Lens multiplier factor (LMF): Also known as 'focal length multiplier' or 'lens multiplier', this figure describes the ratio of the size of a DSC's sensor to a 35mm frame. It can be calculated by dividing the length, width or diagonal of a 35mm film frame by the equivalent measurement on the DSC's sensor. This ratio is commonly quoted for interchangeable-lens digital SLR cameras so users can convert the focal lengths of 35mm lenses into their effective equivalents on a digital SLR. Most DSLR LMFs range from 1.5x to 2x. LMFs are also useful for estimating the depth-of-field capabilities of compact DSCs because they indicate how much more depth-of-field the DSC has at the same lens aperture and subject distance. Most compact digicams have LMFs of between 3.8x and 7.1x.

Linear array: A scanner head system in which red, green and blue photo sensors that produce an image are arranged in a row.

Lossless compression: A compression technique that allows smaller files to be created without sacrificing the original data values.

Lossy compression: A compression technique in which smaller files are produced by eliminating some of the original data. It produces smaller files than lossless compression and users can normally control how much data is sacrificed.

Luminance: The intensity or brightness of an image, determined by the amount of grey in a hue. (Also known as 'lightness'.)

Megabyte (MB): 1,048,576 bytes of computer memory.

Metadata: Structured data, stored with digital image files, which explains, locates, describes or otherwise makes using the original primary data more effective or efficient. Two types of metadata are important for digital camera users: the Exif standard and the digital print order format (DPOF) standard, which was developed by an industry group representing Canon, Kodak, Fujifilm and Matsushita (Panasonic).

Motion JPEG: A type of AVI file format that handles images and sound as a single file, recording images in JPEG format. Motion JPEG can be played back by QuickTime 3.0 or later.

MPEG: A family of video compression standards developed by the Motion Picture Experts Group. MPEG-1 is commonly used for CD video applications, while MPEG-2 is designed for inter-laced and progressive scan video and is popular for a wide range of video applications. MPEG-3 was designed for HDTV but is seldom (if ever) used. MPEG-4 has evolved from the earlier standards but is designed for a broader range of multimedia applications. It is offered in some digicams with VGA video capture capability.

Noise: Defects in an image resulting from electronic interference or errors in the camera's digital signal processing systems.

Non-linear editing: An editing process in which video clips are selected and arranged on a computer using dedicated software. The clips are not recorded permanently during the editing process but cut-in and cut-out points are stored as digital markers in the computer's memory. This makes it easy to locate recorded segments and editors can instantly check their work and make adjustments. When the sequence is finalised, an 'edit decision list' is stored in the computer's memory and the final edited video is transferred to videotape or an optical medium like CD or DVD.

Optical resolution: The maximum physical (non-interpolated) resolution provided by a device. The term is commonly applied to scanners.

Optical zoom: The maximum zoom range achievable with the camera's lens. Image quality is fully maintained.

Orientation: The direction in which a page is printed or an image is viewed: landscape is printed horizontally, while portrait is printed vertically. Some cameras can automatically rotate photographs taken in portrait format to present them the right way up for viewing on the LCD screen.

Photodiode/photosite: A photodiode is a light-sensitive cell on a digital image sensor, while the term 'photosite' refers to the photodiode plus the overlying microlens and colour filter. Each photosite records one intensity and one colour value. Information from several photosites is required to create a pixel in an image.

Pixel: Short for 'picture element', this term describes the basic component of a digital image. Individual pixels are generally square and carry one value for colour, luminance and intensity. Millions of pixels are required to produce a digital image that approaches photographic quality.

Posterisation: An editing process that reduces the number of tones in an image, creating a simplified and often surreal effect.

Prosumer is a term commonly applied to products that sit between the professional and consumer markets.

Primary colour: A colour that forms the basis for all other colour combinations. The three primary colours of light (also known as 'additive primaries') are red, green and blue, while for colour printing, the three ('subtractive') primary colours are cyan, magenta and yellow.

QuickTime: A popular video codec (coding/decoding system) denoted by the *.mov filename extension. It was developed for displaying digital video on a computer screen and was initially targeted at Apple PCs but QuickTime files can now be displayed by other operating systems. The required QuickTime player can be downloaded free of charge from www.apple.com.

QVGA (quarter video graphics display), QQVGA (quarter quarter video graphics display): Shorthand terms used to describe video resolutions of 320 x 240 pixels and 160 x 120 pixels respectively.

Raw data: Digital information that has not been processed or formatted. Many high-end digital cameras provide a RAW capture option, most using proprietary file formats that require special software to be decoded. No standard file extension has been adopted for RAW files. Because they are unprocessed, RAW files are effectively 'digital negatives' that photographers can adjust as they please. When converted into TIFF files, most give two bit-depth options: 8-bit and 16-bit.

Resolution: The ability to reproduce fine detail. In digital imaging, this is generally defined by the number of pixels obtained from the camera's sensor or in the resulting image.

RGB: A colour model based on the red, green and blue components in the output, it is typically used for images that are captured by digital cameras and displayed on monitors.

Saturation: The intensity of a hue. Pastels have low saturation, while bright colours are highly saturated.

Sharpening: An image enhancement technique that uses software to give more distinct edges to subject areas, lines and tones in an image.

Sharpening artefacts: These are defects introduced by over-sharpening. They generally appear as white or black halos around high-contrast areas in the subject and can sometimes be minimised by turning off the auto sharpening function in the camera.

sRGB: The standard colour space used by digital cameras, camcorders, TV and computer monitors, scanners and printing systems and supported by all image editing software. Its colour gamut is not quite as wide as Adobe RGB, which is available in most digital SLRs and prosumer DSCs.

Subtractive primary colours: The three colours used to create all other colours when images are printed, they consist of cyan, magenta and yellow.

Thumbnail: A reduced-size, low-resolution version of a digital image, used mainly for sorting and retrieving image files.

Tagged image file format (TIFF): An image file format based on bitmapping that involves little or no data compression. Denoted by the *.tif extension.

Tungsten lighting: Light produced by either photofloods or domestic light bulbs, it has a Kelvin value of 3200 and is warmer than normal daylight.

TWAIN: A standard application protocol that allows computers to interact with devices like digital cameras and scanners. Driver software is required for each device.

Universal serial bus (USB): The most common way of connecting a peripheral device to a computer, USB offers 'hot' plug-and-play (you don't need to switch off the PC). The latest version, USB 2.0 Hi-Speed, which can transmit data at up to 480 Mbits/second, is 40 times faster than the standard USB 1.1 maximum of 12 Mbits/second. A special driver is required to enable the USB 2.0 Hi-Speed to achieve its high transfer rates.

Video graphics array (VGA): A video monitor with mid-level (640 x 480 pixels) resolution. Also applied to 640 x 480 pixel images.

WAVE (waveform audio): A standard Windows format for saving audio data, denoted by the *.wav file extension. WAVE files can be either compressed or uncompressed and can be played back with Windows MediaPlayer or QuickTime 3.0 (or later) software.

White balance: The control on a digital camera used to adjust the colour balance of the image to make shots look natural under a variety of different lighting conditions. Most cameras have presets for tungsten and fluorescent room lighting plus daylight and open shade. A few also include a flash setting. Virtually all digital cameras have an auto white balance setting.

Zoom: A camera or software control that causes the image or part of it to appear larger (zooming in) or smaller (zooming out).

Appendix 1

Memory card capacities and approximate prices in A$ (as of October 2004)

Card type	64 MB	128 MB	256 MB
CF Type 1	$16-$59	$25-$69	$35-$106
CF Type II	$17-$60	$25-$79	$39-$119
High-Speed CF	n.a.	n.a.	$50-$200
Memory Stick	$29-$119	$39-$159	$60-$159
Memory Stick PRO	n.a.	$72-$169	$59-$169
Memory Stick Duo	$59-$159	$75-$179	$99-$179
Memory Stick Pro Duo	n.a	$45-$180	$59-$226
SD	$35-$69	$39-$89	$39-$189
MMC	$24-$65	$29-$89	$39-$135
SmartMedia	$39-$60	$59-$108	n.a.
xD Picture Card	$29-$65	$39-$132	$67-$245

* 'n.a.' indicates that this capacity is not currently available for this type of card. This situation may change as card capacities increase.

Note: CompactFlash cards have been released with 8 GB and 12 GB capacities but local prices were not available when we went to press.

512 MB	1 GB	2 GB	4 GB
$55-$129	$97-$309	$179-$585	$599-$699
$57-$159	$97-$340	$179-$599	$769-$899
$69-$340	$115-$540	$209-$604	$450-$999
n.a.	n.a.	n.a.	n.a
$99-$379	$199-$649	$369-$899	n.a
$439	n.a.	n.a.	n.a.
$107-$411	n.a.	n.a.	n.a.
$59-$299	$99-$380	n.a.	n.a.
$69-$187	$149-$220	n.a.	n.a.
n.a.	n.a.	n.a.	n.a.
$115-$350	n.a.	n.a.	n.a.

How many JPEG pictures can you store?

Approximate number of high-resolution images per capacity

Camera type:	File size*	32MB	64MB	128MB
2-megapixel camera:	800–900KB	35–40	70–80	140–160
3-megapixel camera:	1.0–1.2MB	26–32	53–64	106–128
4-megapixel camera:	1.8–2MB	16–18	32–35	64–71
5-megapixel camera:	2.0–2.5MB	12–16	25–32	51–64
6-megapixel camera:	2.8–3.2MB	10–11	20–22	40–45

* Average file size range using a typical camera's high-resolution JPEG mode. The actual number of images per card will be dictated by the compression ratios applied by the camera and the complexity of the scene being photographed.

256MB	512MB	1GB	2GB	4GB
284–320	568–640	1137–1280	2275–2570	4551–5119
213–256	426–512	853–1024	1706–2056	3413–4096
128–142	256–284	512–568	1024–1137	2048–2275
102–128	204–256	409–512	819–1024	1638–2048
80–91	160–182	320–365	640–731	1280–1462

Appendix 2

Sensor dimensions for digital cameras

The table below shows the physical dimensions of the most commonly used sensors in compact DSCs and under-$4000 DSLR cameras. The dimensions of a 35mm film frame are provided for comparison.

Sensor 'type'	Width (mm)	Height (mm)	Diagonal (mm)
1/3.6-inch	4.0	3.0	5.0
1/3.2-inch	4.54	3.41	5.68
1/3-inch	4.8	3.6	6.0
1/2.5-inch	5.34	4.01	6.1
1/2.7-inch	5.27	3.96	6.59
1/2-inch	6.4	4.8	8.0
1/1.8-inch	7.18	5.32	8.93
2/3-inch	8.8	6.6	11.03
1-inch	12.8	9.6	16.0
4/3-inch	18.0	13.5	22.5
Canon CMOS	22.7	15.1	27.26
'APS-C' CCD	23.7	15.6	28.37
35mm film	36.0	24.0	43.3

Photosite areas for digital cameras

The table below shows the dimensions of individual photosites for a selection of the most popular sensor sizes for compact DSCs and DSLRs, with representative cameras using each sensor type.

Sensor 'type'	Effective resolution	Photosite area (μm)	Representative cameras
1/2.5-inch	4-megapixel	2.32 x 2.32	Kodak DX7440
1/2.5-inch	5-megapixel	2.09 x 2.09	Pentax Optio S5i
1/2.7-inch	3-megapixel	2.6 x 2.6	Olympus C-370 Zoom
1/2.7-inch	4-megapixel	2.32 x 2.32	Fujifilm FinePix S3500
1/1.8-inch	4-megapixel	3.13 x 3.13	Nikon Coolpix 5200
1/1.8-inch	6-megapixel	2. 54 x 2.54	Casio QV-R61
2/3-inch	8-megapixel	2.70 x 2.70	Konica Minolta DiMAGE A2
4/3-inch	5-megapixel	6.80 x 6.80	Olympus E-1
22.7 x 15.1mm	6.3-megapixel	7.4 x 7.4	Canon EOS 300D
23.7 x 15.6mm	6.1-megapixel	7.8 x 7.8	Nikon D70, Pentax *ist DS

Appendix 3

Digital Imaging Equipment Distributors

CANON

Canon Australia Consumer Imaging Products Group
1 Thomas Holt Drive
North Ryde NSW 2113
Ph: 1800 021 167
www.canon.com.au

Canon New Zealand Ltd
PO Box 33–336
Takapuna Auckland
Ph: 0800 222 666
www.canon.co.nz

EPSON

Epson Australia
3 Talavera Road
North Ryde NSW 2113
Ph: 1300 131 928
www.epson.com.au

Epson New Zealand
Epson House
Level 4 245 Hobson St Auckland
Ph: 09 366 6855
www.epson.co.nz

FUJIFILM
Fujifilm Australia
114 Old Pittwater Road
Brookvale NSW 2100
Ph: 1800 226 355
www.fujifilm.com.au

Fujifilm New Zealand
PO Box 101 500
North Shore Mail Centre Auckland
Ph: 09 414 0400
www.fujifilm.co.nz

HEWLETT-PACKARD
Hewlett-Packard Australia Pty Ltd
31–41 Joseph Street
Blackburn VIC 3130
Ph: 131 347
www.hp.com.au

HP New Zealand
HP House
4 Viaduct Harbour Avenue
Maritime Square Auckland 1001
Ph: 09 918 9555
www.hp.co.nz

KODAK
Kodak Australasia
173 Elizabeth Street
Coburg VIC 3058
Ph: 1800 147701
wwwau.kodak.com

Kodak New Zealand
POBox 2198 Auckland
Ph: 09 302 8610
wwwnz.kodak.com

KONICA MINOLTA
Konica Minolta Photo Imaging Australia
22 Giffnock Avenue
North Ryde NSW 2113
Ph: (02) 9878 5333
www.konicaminolta.com.au

Konica Minolta Business Solutions New Zealand
34 Vestey Drive
Mt Wellington Auckland
Ph: 09 573 5450
www.konicaminolta.co.nz

KYOCERA
Tasco Australia
9–13 Winbourne Road
Brookvale NSW 2100
Ph. (02) 9938 3244
www.tasco.com.au

Kyocera Mita New Zealand Ltd.
1–3 Parkhead Place
Albany Auckland 1330
Ph. 0800 451 000
www.kyoceramita.co.nz

LEICA
Adeal Pty Ltd
2 Baldwin Road
Altona VIC 3025
Ph: 03 8369 4444
www.adeal.com.au

Lacklands Limited
48 George Street
Mt Eden Auckland 3
Ph: 09 630 0753
www.lacklands.co.nz

NIKON
Maxwell Optical Industries
Unit F1 Lidcombe Business Park
23 Birnie Avenue
Lidcombe NSW 2141
Ph: 1300 366 499
www.maxwell.com.au

TA Macalister Ltd
65–73 Parnell Rise
Auckland New Zealand
Ph: 09 303 4334
www.macalister.co.nz

OLYMPUS
Olympus Australia
82 Waterloo Road
North Ryde NSW 2113
Ph: 1300 659 678
www.olympus.com.au

Olympus New Zealand
27D Waipareira Avenue
Henderson Auckland
Ph: 09 836 9993
www.olympus.co.nz

PANASONIC

Panasonic Australia
Austlink Corporate Park
1 Garigal RoadBelrose NSW 2085
Ph: 132 600
www.panasonic.com.au

Panasonic New Zealand
350 Te Irirangi Drive
East Tamaki Auckland
Ph: 09 272 0100
www.panasonic.co.nz

PENTAX

C R Kennedy & Company
663 Chapel Street
South Yarra VIC 3141
Ph: 03 9823 1555
www.crkennedy.com.au

C R Kennedy (NZ) Ltd
Unit 2 No 3 Hotunui Drive
Mt Wellington Auckland
Ph: 09 276 8618
www.crknz.co.nz

RICOH

Ricoh Australia Pty Ltd
148 Highbury Road
Burwood VIC 3125
Ph: 1300 363 741
www.ricoh.com.au

Ricoh New Zealand
Level 2 60 Stanley Street
Parnell Auckland
Ph: 0800 274 264
www.ricoh.co.nz

SAMSUNG

Adeal Pty Ltd
2 Baldwin Road
Altona VIC 3025
Ph: (03) 8369 4444
www.adeal.com.au

C R Kennedy (NZ) Ltd
Unit 2 No 3 Hotunui Drive
Mt Wellington Auckland
Ph: 09 276 8618
www.crknz.co.nz

SONY

Sony Australia
33–39 Talavera Road
North Ryde NSW 2113
Ph: 1300 137 669
www.sony.com.au

Sony New Zealand Ltd
Akoranga Business Park
Northcote Auckland
Ph: 09 488 6188
www.sony.co.nz

Index